ROYAL COURT

Royal Court Theatre presents

MOTHER TERESA IS DEAD

by **Helen Edmundson**

First performance at the Royal Court Jerwood Theatre Upstairs
Sloane Square, London on 20 June 2002.

Supported by the Royal Court's Production Syndicate scheme.

MOTHER TERESA IS DEAD

by **Helen Edmundson**

Cast in order of appearance
Frances **Diana Quick**
Mark **John Marquez**
Srinivas **Harry Dillon**
Jane **Maxine Peake**

Director **Simon Usher**
Designer **Anthony Lamble**
Lighting Designer **Paul Russell**
Sound Designer **Ian Dickinson**
Casting Director **Lisa Makin**
Production Manager **Sue Bird**
Company Stage Manager **Cath Binks**
Stage Management **Louise McDermott, Jo Spooner**
Student Work Placement **Graeme Brown**
Costume Supervisor **Iona Kenrick**
Wardrobe Mistress **Jackie Orton**
Dialect Coach **Jeanette Nelson**
Company Voice Work **Patsy Rodenburg**

Royal Court Theatre would like to thank the following for their help with this production:
Evelyn Williams, Richard Harris, Paul Bhattacharjee, Kausalya Santhanam. Wardrobe care by Persil and
Comfort courtesy of Lever Fabergé.

THE COMPANY

Helen Edmundson (writer)
Theatre includes: Flying (RNT Studio); The Clearing (Bush/national & international productions). Adaptations include: Anna Karenina (Shared Experience, Tricycle/Lyric Hammersmith/national & international tours and productions); Mill on the Floss (Shared Experience, Tricycle/Lyric Hammersmith/national & international tours and productions); War and Peace (Shared Experience at the RNT).
Film and Television includes: The Clearing (for production 2003), The Spire.
Awards include: John Whiting Award for The Clearing, Time Out Theatre Awards for Mill On the Floss and The Clearing and TMA Award for Anna Karenina.

Ian Dickinson (sound designer)
For the Royal Court: Push Up, Workers Writes, F***ing Games, Herons, Cutting Through the Carnival.
Other theatre includes: Night of the Soul (RSC Barbican); Eyes of the Kappa (Gate); Crime and Punishment in Dalston (Arcola Theatre); Search and Destroy (New End, Hampstead); Phaedra, Three Sisters, The Shaughraun, Writer's Cramp (Royal Lyceum, Edinburgh); The Whore's Dream (RSC Fringe, Edinburgh); As You Like It, An Experienced Woman Gives Advice, Present Laughter, The Philadelphia Story, Wolks World, Poor Superman, Martin Yesterday, Fast Food, Coyote Ugly, Prizenight (Royal Exchange, Manchester); Great Monsters of Western Street (Throat Theatre Company); Small Craft Warnings, Tieble and Her Demon (Manchester Evening News Theatre Awards Best Design Team), The Merchant of Venice, Death and The Maiden (Library Theatre Company, Manchester).
Ian is Acting Head of Sound at the Royal Court.

Harry Dillon
Theatre includes: As You Like It (Jermyn Street); The House of Desires (BAC); Franziska (Gate).
Television includes: Thief Takers, Dream Team, Arabian Nights, The Score, Trial and Retribution, Headless, Holby City.
Film includes: Eleven One Ninety Seven, New World Disorder, Entrapment, Wit, The Lawless Heart, State of the Party, Cradle 2 The Grave.

Anthony Lamble (designer)
For the Royal Court: Herons.
Other theatre includes: The Roman Actor (RSC); Sing Yer Heart Out For The Lads (RNT); Comedians, The Contractor, Troilus and Cressida (Oxford Stage Company); A Christmas Carol (Chichester Festival); A Midsummer Night's Dream, As You Like It (RNT and tour); In Celebration, The Sea, Aristocrats, The Retreat from Moscow, The School of Night, Insignificance, The King of Prussia, Spell of Cold Weather (Minerva, Chichester); Barefoot in the Park (Watford Palace/Northampton Theatre Royal); Lettice and Lovage, Burning Everest, Exquisite Sister (West Yorkshire Playhouse); Card Boys, All of You Mine, Mortal Ash, Pond Life, Not Fade Away, Evil Doers, Looking at You (Revived Again) (Bush); Pippin, Biloxi Blues, The Odd Couple, Dancing at Lughnasa (NYT/ Arts); Heartbreak House, Hamlet, Whole Lotta Shakin', Comedians (Belgrade). Anthony has also designed productions for Leicester Haymarket, Sheffield Crucible, Almeida Music Festival, English Touring Theatre, The Gate, Riverside Studios, Lyric Hammersmith, Shared Experience, Paines Plough and RSC Pit.
Dance and Opera includes: Facing Viv (English National Ballet's Tour De Force); Palace in the Sky (Hackney Empire for the ENO/Lilian Baylis Programme); L'Orfeo (Purcell Quartet, Japanese tour).
Film includes: A Secret Audience.
Anthony is a course tutor for the Motley Theatre Design Course.

John Marquez
For the Royal Court: Local (Exposure, Young Writers Festival).
Other theatre includes: Sing Yer Heart Out For The Lads (RNT); Snowbull (Hampstead); From Street Car to Tennessee (Young Vic); Baby Doll (RNT & West End); Small Craft Warnings (Pleasance); The Colonel Bird (Gate); Romeo and Juliet (Greenwich); The End of the Affair (Salisbury).
Television includes: Soldier, Soldier, Killing Me Softly, The Bill, Eastenders, Black Books.

Maxine Peake

Theatre includes: Luther, The Relapse, The Cherry Orchard (RNT); Miss Julie (Theatre Royal, Haymarket); Early One Morning (Bolton Octagon).

Television and film includes: Dalziel and Pascoe, All or Nothing, The Way We Live Now, Victoria Wood with all the Trimmings, Dinner Ladies (series 1 & 2), Clocking Off, Jonathan Creek, Girls Night, Hetty Wainthrop Investigates.

Diana Quick

For the Royal Court: The Old Neighborhood, Lear, The Sea.

Other theatre includes: Ghosts (ETT); Be My Baby, Kindertransport (Soho); Hamlet, The Woman Pirates, The Changeling (RSC); A Map of the World, Tamburlaine, Troilus and Cressida, Plunder, Phaedra Britannica (RNT); Fly Away Home, Progress, The Women Destroyed (Lyric Hammersmith); The Women (Old Vic); If We Were Women, Mindkill (Greenwich); Rough Justice, Billy, Threepenny Opera (West End).

Television includes: Dalziel & Pascoe (new series), The Aristocrats, Under The Sun, September Song, Dandelion Dead, Inspector Morse, Inspector Alleyn, Clarissa, The Orchid House, The Justice Game, Chekov in Yalta, Carianni and the Courtesans, The Woman in White, Brideshead Revisited, The Three Hostages, Mr Garrick & Mrs Woffington, Napoleon in Love, The Best Things in Life.

Film includes: The Discovery of Heaven, A.K.A., The Revenger's Tragedy, The Affair of the Necklace, Vigo: Burning Up, Nostradamus, Wilt, Vroom, Max Mon Amour, 1919, Ordeal by Innocence, The Duellists, The Big Sleep, The Odd Job, Nicholas and Alexandra.

Paul Russell (lighting designer)

For the Royal Court: Herons, Not a Game for Boys.

Other theatre includes: The Fall (Young Vic); Hard Times (Watermill, Newbury); Closer (RNT international tour); Madame Butterfly (Singapore Repertory Theatre); Trainspotting, Raising Fires, One Flea Spare (amongst many other productions at the Bush); The Way You Look Tonight (Druid); Exodus (Tara Arts); The Cherry Orchard (Guildhall); Danton's Death, The Portuguese Boat Plays, The Great Highway, Rousseau's Tale, Bad Blood, Picnic /Guernica, Talking Tongues, Anowa, Dear Elena Sergeievna, Silver Face, Hunting Scenes in Lower Bavaria (Gate); Madness in Valencia, The Great Pretenders (Gate and tour); Fat Janet, Iona Rain (Croydon Warehouse); Peribanez (Cambridge Arts); The Wolves (Paines Plough tour); My Mother Said I Never Should (Oxford Stage Co); Yiddish Trojan Woman (Cockpit); Boy (Everyman Liverpool/Lyric Hammersmith/BAC and national tour); Love at a Loss (BAC and national tour); Mr Director (Orange Tree); Theaker Dance (Palace and tour); Webster (Old Red Lion); The Eleventh Commandment (Hampstead); Max Clapper (Electric Cinema); Exquisite Sister (West Yorkshire Playhouse/ Edinburgh Festival); Musical Scenes (BAC); Pig's Ear (Liverpool Playhouse).

Opera includes: Snatched by the Gods, Broken Strings (Almeida), Linda Di Chamonix, Rape of Lucretia (Guildhall), Cosi Fan Tutti (Ealing), West Side Story (Pimlico Opera at Wandsworth Prison).

Paul is Resident Production Manager at the Young Vic.

Simon Usher (director)

For the Royal Court: Herons.

Other theatre includes: Sing Yer Heart Out For The Lads (RNT); Musicians Crossing A Bridge Without Their Instruments (Dial Theatre); Looking at You (Revived) Again, The Evil Doers, Pond Life, Not Fade Away, The Mortal Ash, All of You Mine, Wishbones, Card Boys (Bush); King Baby (RSC, Pit); The War in Heaven, Timon of Athens, Pericles, The Winter's Tale, The Broken Heart, The Lover's Melancholy, French Without Tears, The Bells, Pale Performer, Trios, Lettice and Lovage, The Naked, Murders in the Rue Morgue (Haymarket, Leicester); Waiting for Godot, The Browning Version, Heartbreak House, Hamlet, Les Liaisons Dangereuses, Whole Lotta Shakin' (Belgrade, Coventry); No Man's Land (English Touring Theatre); Mr Puntila and His Man Matti (Chichester); Can't Stand Up for Falling Down (Watford Palace and tour); Burning Everest, Exquisite Sister (West Yorkshire Playhouse); The Wolves (Paines Plough); Twins (Birmingham Rep); Great Balls of Fire (Cambridge Theatre, West End).

THE ENGLISH STAGE COMPANY AT THE ROYAL COURT

The English Stage Company at the Royal Court opened in 1956 as a subsidised theatre producing new British plays, international plays and some classical revivals.

The first artistic director George Devine aimed to create a writers' theatre, 'a place where the dramatist is acknowledged as the fundamental creative force in the theatre and where the play is more important than the actors, the director, the designer'. The urgent need was to find a contemporary style in which the play, the acting, direction and design are all combined. He believed that 'the battle will be a long one to continue to create the right conditions for writers to work in'.

Devine aimed to discover 'hard-hitting, uncompromising writers whose plays are stimulating, provocative and exciting'. The Royal Court production of John Osborne's Look Back in Anger in May 1956 is now seen as the decisive starting point of modern British drama and the policy created a new generation of British playwrights. The first wave included John Osborne, Arnold Wesker, John Arden, Ann Jellicoe, N F Simpson and Edward Bond. Early seasons included new international plays by Bertolt Brecht, Eugène Ionesco, Samuel Beckett, Jean-Paul Sartre and Marguerite Duras.

The theatre started with the 400-seat proscenium arch Theatre Downstairs, and then in 1969 opened a second theatre, the 60-seat studio Theatre Upstairs. Some productions transfer to the West End, such as Caryl Churchill's Far Away, Conor McPherson's The Weir, Kevin Elyot's Mouth to Mouth and My Night With Reg. The Royal Court also co-produces plays which have transferred to the West End or toured internationally, such as Sebastian Barry's The Steward of Christendom and Mark Ravenhill's Shopping and Fucking (with Out of Joint), Martin McDonagh's The Beauty Queen Of Leenane (with Druid Theatre Company), Ayub Khan-Din's East is East (with Tamasha Theatre Company, and now a feature film).

Since 1994 the Royal Court's artistic policy has again been vigorously directed to finding and producing a new generation of playwrights. The writers include Joe Penhall, Rebecca Prichard, Michael Wynne, Nick Grosso, Judy Upton, Meredith Oakes, Sarah Kane, Anthony Neilson, Judith Johnson, James Stock, Jez Butterworth, Marina Carr, Phyllis Nagy, Simon Block, Martin McDonagh, Mark Ravenhill, Ayub Khan-Din, Tamantha Hammerschlag, Jess Walters, Che Walker, Conor McPherson, Simon Stephens,

photo: Andy Chopping

Richard Bean, Roy Williams, Gary Mitchell, Mick Mahoney, Rebecca Gilman, Christopher Shinn, Kia Corthron, David Gieselmann, Marius von Mayenburg, David Eldridge, Leo Butler, Zinnie Harris, Grae Cleugh, Roland Schimmelpfennig and Vassily Sigarev. This expanded programme of new plays has been made possible through the support of A.S.K Theater Projects, the Jerwood Charitable Foundation, the American Friends of the Royal Court Theatre and many in association with the Royal National Theatre Studio.

In recent years there have been record-breaking productions at the box office, with capacity houses for Jez Butterworth's The Night Heron, Rebecca Gilman's Boy Gets Girl, Kevin Elyot's Mouth To Mouth, David Hare's My Zinc Bed and Conor McPherson's The Weir, which transferred to the West End in October 1998 and ran for nearly two years at the Duke of York's Theatre.

The newly refurbished theatre in Sloane Square opened in February 2000, with a policy still inspired by the first artistic director George Devine. The Royal Court is an international theatre for new plays and new playwrights, and the work shapes contemporary drama in Britain and overseas.

AWARDS FOR
THE ROYAL COURT

Terry Johnson's Hysteria won the 1994 Olivier Award for Best Comedy, and also the Writers' Guild Award for Best West End Play. Kevin Elyot's My Night with Reg won the 1994 Writers' Guild Award for Best Fringe Play, the Evening Standard Award for Best Comedy, and the 1994 Olivier Award for Best Comedy. Joe Penhall was joint winner of the 1994 John Whiting Award for Some Voices. Sebastian Barry won the 1995 Writers' Guild Award for Best Fringe Play, the Critics' Circle Award and the 1995 Lloyds Private Banking Playwright of the Year Award for The Steward of Christendom. Jez Butterworth won the 1995 George Devine Award, the Writers' Guild New Writer of the Year Award, the Evening Standard Award for Most Promising Playwright and the Olivier Award for Best Comedy for Mojo.

The Royal Court was the overall winner of the 1995 Prudential Award for the Arts for creativity, excellence, innovation and accessibility. The Royal Court Theatre Upstairs won the 1995 Peter Brook Empty Space Award for innovation and excellence in theatre.

Michael Wynne won the 1996 Meyer-Whitworth Award for The Knocky. Martin McDonagh won the 1996 George Devine Award, the 1996 Writers' Guild Best Fringe Play Award, the 1996 Critics' Circle Award and the 1996 Evening Standard Award for Most Promising Playwright for The Beauty Queen of Leenane. Marina Carr won the 19th Susan Smith Blackburn Prize (1996/7) for Portia Coughlan. Conor McPherson won the 1997 George Devine Award, the 1997 Critics' Circle Award and the 1997 Evening Standard Award for Most Promising Playwright for The Weir. Ayub Khan-Din won the 1997 Writers' Guild Awards for Best West End Play and Writers' Guild New Writer of the Year and the 1996 John Whiting Award for East is East (co-production with Tamasha).

At the 1998 Tony Awards, Martin McDonagh's The Beauty Queen of Leenane (co-production with Druid Theatre Company) won four awards including Garry Hynes for Best Director and was nominated for a further two. Eugene Ionesco's The Chairs (co-production with Theatre de Complicite) was nominated for six Tony awards. David Hare won the 1998 Time Out Live Award for Outstanding Achievement and six awards in New York including the Drama League, Drama Desk and New York Critics Circle Award for Via Dolorosa. Sarah Kane won the 1998 Arts Foundation Fellowship in Playwriting. Rebecca Prichard won the 1998 Critics' Circle Award for Most Promising Playwright for Yard Gal (co-production with Clean Break).

Conor McPherson won the 1999 Olivier Award for Best New Play for The Weir. The Royal Court won the 1999 ITI Award for Excellence in International Theatre. Sarah Kane's Cleansed was judged Best Foreign Language Play in 1999 by Theater Heute in Germany. Gary Mitchell won the 1999 Pearson Best Play Award for Trust. Rebecca Gilman was joint winner of the 1999 George Devine Award and won the 1999 Evening Standard Award for Most Promising Playwright for The Glory of Living.

Roy Williams and Gary Mitchell were joint winners of the George Devine Award 2000 for Most Promising Playwright for Lift Off and The Force of Change respectively. At the Barclays Theatre Awards 2000 presented by the TMA, Richard Wilson won the Best Director Award for David Gieselmann's Mr Kolpert and Jeremy Herbert won the Best Designer Award for Sarah Kane's 4.48 Psychosis. Gary Mitchell won the Evening Standard's Charles Wintour Award 2000 for Most Promising Playwright for The Force of Change. Stephen Jeffreys' I Just Stopped by to See The Man won an AT&T: On Stage Award 2000. David Eldridge's Under the Blue Sky won the Time Out Live Award 2001 for Best New Play in the West End. Leo Butler won the George Devine Award 2001 for Most Promising Playwright for Redundant. Roy Williams won the Evening Standard's Charles Wintour Award 2001 for Most Promising Playwright for Clubland. Grae Cleugh won the 2001 Olivier Award for Most Promising Playwright for Fucking Games.

In 1999, the Royal Court won the European theatre prize New Theatrical Realities, presented at Taormina Arte in Sicily, for its efforts in recent years in discovering and producing the work of young British dramatists.

ROYAL COURT BOOKSHOP

The bookshop offers a wide range of playtexts and theatre books, with over 1,000 titles. Located in the downstairs Bar and Food area, the bookshop is open Monday to Saturday, afternoons and evenings.

Many Royal Court playtexts are available for just £2 including works by Harold Pinter, Caryl Churchill, Rebecca Gilman, Martin Crimp, Sarah Kane, Conor McPherson, Ayub Khan-Din, Timberlake Wertenbaker and Roy Williams.

For information on titles and special events, Email: bookshop@royalcourttheatre.com
Tel: 020 7565 5024

REBUILDING THE ROYAL COURT

In 1995, the Royal Court was awarded a National Lottery grant through the Arts Council of England, to pay for three quarters of a £26m project to completely rebuild its 100-year old home. The rules of the award required the Royal Court to raise £7.6m in partnership funding. The building has been completed thanks to the generous support of those listed below.

We are particularly grateful for the contributions of over 5,700 audience members.

English Stage Company Registered Charity number 231242.

THE AMERICAN FRIENDS OF THE ROYAL COURT THEATRE

AFRCT support the mission of the Royal Court and are primarily focused on raising funds to enable the theatre to produce new work by emerging American writers. Since this not-for-profit organisation was founded in 1997, AFRCT has contributed to eight productions including Christopher Shinn's Where Do We Live. They have also supported the participation of young artists in the Royal Court's acclaimed International Residency.

If you would like to support the ongoing work of the Royal Court, please contact the Development Department on 020 7565 5050.

THE ARTS COUNCIL OF ENGLAND

PROGRAMME SUPPORTERS

The Royal Court (English Stage Company Ltd) receives its principal funding from London Arts. It is also supported financially by a wide range of private companies and public bodies and earns the remainder of its income from the box office and its own trading activities.
The Royal Borough of Kensington & Chelsea gives an annual grant to the Royal Court Young Writers' Programme and the Affiliation of London Government provides project funding for a number of play development initiatives.

The Jerwood Charitable Foundation continues to support new plays by new playwrights through the Jerwood New Playwrights series. Since 1993 the A.S.K. Theater Projects of Los Angeles has funded a Playwrights' Programme at the theatre. Bloomberg Mondays, the Royal Court's reduced price ticket scheme, is supported by Bloomberg. Over the past seven years the BBC has supported the Gerald Chapman Fund for directors.

FOR THE ROYAL COURT

MOTHER TERESA IS DEAD

Characters

FRANCES

MARK

SRINIVAS

JANE

ACT ONE

Scene One

*The living room of a house, in a village near Madras, Southern
India. It has wooden floors and white plaster walls and there
are several exits leading from it. There is an eclectic range
of chairs and sofas roughly grouped around a coffee-table.
At least one of the chairs is very low and well-worn. There are
several decorative cushions and a colourful rug.*

*The light in the room is beautiful; strong sunlight, gracefully
filtered and deflected. The overall atmosphere is open,
uncluttered and calm.*

*The sound of a brass door-knocker against heavy wood is
heard, off. After a few moments it is repeated. Then, just
audible, the sound of a door being opened and closed.*

A woman enters, followed by a man.

*The woman is in her mid-fifties. She wears simple, light, plain
clothes and no make-up. She has the sort of looks which cause
people to say 'she must have been beautiful when she was
young'. In fact she is still beautiful, though there is a habitual
sadness in her expression. She works hard to overcome the
shyness and uncertainty she feels in dealing with strangers.*

*The man is in his early thirties. He is carrying a holdall and
clutching a piece of paper with an address written on it. He is
wearing a polo shirt, jeans and a jacket and is drenched in
sweat. He is anxious and strained. When he speaks, he has a
strong London accent.*

FRANCES. Come through. It's Mark, isn't it?

MARK. Yes.

FRANCES. I'm Frances. You found it all right, then?

MARK. Yes.

MARK *is looking around the room.*

FRANCES. That's good. You can get the odd taxi-driver who doesn't know this village. I am a little off the beaten track.

MARK. She is here, isn't she?

FRANCES. Yes. Yes, she is here.

MARK. So where is she?

FRANCES. She's sleeping at the moment. In the garden. She's having trouble sleeping at night and she tends to catch up in the day. I try not to wake her.

MARK *is looking angry and disappointed.*

I will though, if you want me to.

Pause. MARK *does not reply.*

Let me get you something to drink.

MARK. Does she know I'm coming?

FRANCES. Yes. Yes, she knows. Lime soda, would that be all right? It's homemade. It's the best thing in this heat.

MARK. Whatever. Thanks.

She exits to the kitchen. MARK *puts his bag down. He stands for a moment and rubs his eyes and the tense muscles in his neck. He chooses a chair out of the sun and sits in it, but immediately regrets his choice – it is too low and soft. He tries another chair, not so shaded, but in which he feels more comfortable. He starts to take his jacket off, and sees the great patches of sweat on his shirt.*

Jesus.

He takes it off anyway, and rolls his sleeves back.

FRANCES (*calling from the kitchen*). Mark?

MARK. Yes?

FRANCES (*calling from the kitchen*). The taxi's still parked at the end of the lane.

MARK. Oh. Right. (*Sarcastically, to himself.*) Great.

FRANCES *enters, carrying a tray with glasses and a jug.*

FRANCES. Did you ask him to wait?

MARK. No. No, to be honest I had to have a word with him.

FRANCES. Oh.

MARK. We had a bust-up. Eight hundred rupees. That's what he wanted. Well I know it isn't round the corner but that's way over the odds, isn't it? I read in the magazine on the plane, it's three hundred rupees from the airport to Madras. So I would have said four hundred. I think four hundred would be about right, wouldn't you?

FRANCES. Well . . .

MARK. Eight hundred rupees is about a week's wages for him, isn't it?

FRANCES. I'm not sure.

MARK. I thought something was up when he turned the meter off at the airport.

FRANCES. It's about ten pounds, I suppose.

MARK. But I didn't know, you know. You don't know when you're in another country, do you? It might just be the way they do it. But he was trying to rip me off because I'd just got off the plane. So I gave him four hundred and he didn't like it.

FRANCES. Right. Yes, I see.

MARK. Do you want me to go and sort it?

FRANCES. No. No, he probably won't wait for long. There are no fares for him around here. If he's still there in ten minutes I'll go and talk to him.

MARK. It's the principle, you know.

FRANCES. Yes.

There is an awkward silence. MARK *takes a long drink. He is sweltering. He wipes his forehead with his sleeve.*

MARK. God, I don't know how anyone stands this.

FRANCES. It is a shock at first.

MARK. Been here a long time have you?

FRANCES. No. Well . . . nearly two years.

MARK. For work, is it? Husband's work?

FRANCES. No. Well, in a way. I paint. I paint pictures.

MARK. Oh.

Pause.

FRANCES. I did live here; when I was a child.

Pause.

No, I've spent most of my life in London.

MARK. Which part?

FRANCES. Hampstead.

MARK (*annoyed*). Nice.

FRANCES. Yes. Shall I find you something cooler to wear?
I've got some *salwars kameez* somewhere – a sort of tunic
and trousers like the Indian men wear.

MARK. I'll manage. Thanks.

Pause.

FRANCES. How was your flight?

MARK. Dreadful.

FRANCES. Oh.

MARK. Full. Disgusting, packing everyone in like that. Like
animals.

FRANCES. Yes. It can be a bit much.

MARK. It took me about three hours to check in. All these
people with great piles of suitcases. Trunks. All their
worldly goods. Aunties. Grannies. Like a travelling circus.
Like a circus.

FRANCES. Oh.

MARK. I have done a long-haul flight before but it was our honeymoon and we were upgraded. Saint Lucia. I didn't know it made such a big difference.

FRANCES. Yes. First class is . . . well, it's very nice if you can do it.

MARK. It's the smell of the food as well. And people's breath, you know. Feet. I was just glad I hadn't got our boy with me. He'd have gone nuts. He hates being cooped up as it is.

FRANCES *is looking at him in surprise.*

There was one woman near me with a baby. New-born. Right carry-on. She shouldn't have brought it anyway. Flying's bad for newborns. It causes cot-death. That's what they say.

FRANCES. Oh.

MARK. You got kids, have you?

FRANCES. Yes. Grown-up ones.

MARK. Still. You don't forget, do you?

Pause.

FRANCES. So, you have a son then?

MARK. Yes. She must have told you. Joe. He's five.

Pause.

She didn't tell you, did she?

FRANCES. No.

MARK. You're sure it's her, are you? You're sure it's Jane?

FRANCES. Yes.

MARK. Taller than average, very dark hair, not short, not long.

FRANCES. Yes. I'm sure it's . . .

MARK (*standing*). I'm going to check.

FRANCES (*assertively*). I'm quite sure it's her. She gave me your telephone number herself. She wanted me to call you.

Pause. MARK *sits again. He is shaken.*

MARK. She didn't say then? About Joe? Didn't mention him?

FRANCES. No. But then she hasn't talked about anything. Not to me. I'm sure it isn't that she's . . .

She trails off.

MARK. What? Forgotten him?

FRANCES. Mark, you have to understand that her state of mind is rather . . . strained.

MARK. What do you mean? Strained? You said she was all right. On the phone. You said she was fine.

FRANCES. Physically she is fine, but . . .

MARK. What's going on? Has someone got to her?

FRANCES. 'Got to her?'

MARK. I mean, is this some sort of cult thing? Or drugs or something? Because if it is, I want to know.

FRANCES. No. No, as far as I know it has nothing to do with anything like . . .

MARK. So what then? You must know something? How did she end up here? Just tell me, will you?

FRANCES. If you stop shouting, I will tell you.

MARK *is silenced. He struggles to control himself.*

The first time I met her, she was with a friend of mine: a man called Srinivas. A charity worker in Madras. He introduced me to Jane. He said she was helping him with his work.

MARK (*amazed*). What?

FRANCES. I saw Srinivas again a few days later and he told me she'd gone. Disappeared without saying anything. He was very worried about her. Then, about five days ago,

I saw her. She was still in Madras. She was in the square
outside the Kapaleeshwara Temple. She was sitting on the
ground. Cross-legged. She was crying. Sort of howling.
There was a small crowd around her. I saw a young man
approach her – a tourist. He bent down and spoke to her but
she didn't respond. I went over to her and asked if she would
like me to help her. She looked up at me. I don't know if
she recognized me or not but at any rate, she nodded. So
I brought her home. Since then she's just rested really.

Pause.

MARK. Wake her up.

FRANCES. Mark . . .

MARK. Wake her up. Now!

He is on his feet, looking for the door to the garden.

FRANCES. Mark, wait, there's something else . . .

MARK. I just want to see my wife, all right!

FRANCES. There's something else I think you should know.
Please listen. For a moment. For a moment.

He stops and looks at her.

When I found her, she didn't have anything with her, as far
as I could tell, except a bag. Just an ordinary white plastic
carrier bag. I picked it up for her, but she snatched it away
from me. She said something about a baby . . . about there
being a baby inside the bag.

MARK. What?

FRANCES. I don't think there is. Well, I'm fairly sure there
isn't. The bag didn't feel heavy enough . . .

MARK. You mean, you haven't looked?

FRANCES. She keeps it with her all the time. Or she hides it.

MARK. Just take it off her and look!

FRANCES. I didn't want to frighten her away.

MARK. Jesus!

FRANCES. There can't be a baby.

MARK. I don't believe this.

FRANCES. If there was it would be dead by now and in this heat . . . well . . .

He is looking at her in horror

But I think something must have happened to her . . . I don't know . . . and she thinks there's a baby. I don't know . . . The day after she arrived here, I came across her in the garden. She was burying the bag in the ground. When she saw me she stopped: she picked it up, brushed the dirt off. That's why I was surprised, when you said she has a son. I suppose I had wondered whether she couldn't have children and she came to India to . . . to find a baby . . .

MARK. She doesn't want any more kids. We have rows about it.

FRANCES. Yes. I see.

Pause.

You don't think there's any chance that she might have . . . that recently she might have been . . .

MARK. What?

Pause. He is staring at her – challenging her to say it.

FRANCES. No. Just thinking aloud.

Pause.

MARK. This bloke she was with?

FRANCES. Srinivas? Yes. Well. He's a good man. He's going to come over today. He's been away. He hasn't seen Jane since I found her.

Long pause.

How long is it since she left home?

MARK. Seven weeks.

FRANCES. And you weren't expecting it at all?

MARK. If I'd been expecting it, I'd have done something
about it, wouldn't I? I'd have stopped her. She just went.
She took Joe to school one morning. I went to work as
usual. The school rang up at the end of the day: she hadn't
turned up to collect him. I went and got him and went home
and . . . She'd left everything very tidy. Cleaned everything.
She'd even left Joe's clothes out for the next day. Laid them
over the back of the red chair. She always did that. I phoned
the police and everything. But they just thought the same
as I did.

FRANCES. What did you think?

MARK. That she'd left. She'd packed some stuff. Taken her
passport. Cash. There was nothing else to think, was there?

FRANCES. But you weren't aware that anything was wrong?

MARK. No. It was just a day.

FRANCES. She hadn't seemed worried or depressed?

MARK. Depressed?

FRANCES. Yes . . .

MARK. You think she's depressed?

FRANCES. I'm not sure. Possibly.

MARK. Her mum gets depressed. She's been on pills since
Jane was a kid. I don't know. It's hard to tell with Jane
sometimes.

FRANCES. What do you mean?

MARK. I don't know. She's got all this stuff in her head, you
know? Then she'll suddenly come out with it all at really
strange times and you just think, Christ, where did all that
come from?

Pause.

Joe started asking for her. At bed-time. He asks for
her every day. I suppose that's what . . . You know, I just
can't . . . (*He fights back his emotion.*) She really loves him.

FRANCES. I'm sure she does.

MARK. We both do. We love him to bits.

He is really agitated by now, embarrassed by his inability to disguise his emotions.

FRANCES. Mark . . .

MARK. Can I use your phone? I want to phone Joe.

FRANCES. I don't have a phone, I'm afraid. There's one in the village.

He is almost in tears.

Mark, would you like to be on your own for a while. I could show you where you can rest, if you like. You must be exhausted . . .

MARK. No. No thanks. I'm not going anywhere 'til I've seen her.

The front door can be heard opening and closing noisily. Footsteps approach.

FRANCES. That must be Srinivas, now.

SRINIVAS *enters. He is Indian, in his late twenties, extremely attractive. He is dressed impeccably in light, european-style clothes. He carries a leather folder and a mobile phone.*

He stops just inside the room and takes in MARK. MARK *stares back at him. There is already an edge of hostility.* FRANCES *stands, about to make introductions –*

SRINIVAS. I just paid your taxi-fare for you.

Pause.

MARK. You did what?

SRINIVAS. He said you owed him four hundred rupees.

MARK. Well, I didn't.

SRINIVAS. He said you did.

MARK. He over-charged me.

SRINIVAS. He said he explained when you got into the taxi
that he would have to charge you double for coming out
here: he has to go all the way back without a fare.

MARK. Yeah, well, I didn't get that.

SRINIVAS. But he did tell you.

MARK. I don't know. He was talking Indian, wasn't he?

SRINIVAS. How very remiss of him.

FRANCES (*quietly*). Vas . . .

*MARK hastily takes some notes out of his pocket and holds
them out to* SRINIVAS.

MARK. Take it.

SRINIVAS. There's no need.

MARK slams the money down on the coffee-table.

MARK. I said, take it!

Pause.

SRINIVAS. Very well.

He picks up the money and puts it in his pocket.

Not for me, you understand. I'll give it to the shelter.

Silence

FRANCES. Srinivas, this is Mark. Mark, this is Srinivas.

The two men stare at each other without speaking.

SRINIVAS *turns away and tosses his things onto a chair.*

I thought you weren't coming until later?

SRINIVAS. I'm not staying long. I had to drive back this way.
I just wanted to make sure she's all right.

FRANCES. She's sleeping. Mark hasn't seen her yet.

SRINIVAS (*to Mark*). You must be very relieved to have found
her.

MARK *says nothing.*

How long has she been away?

MARK *is not going to answer.*

FRANCES. Seven weeks.

SRINIVAS. And you had no idea where she was?

Silence.

Has she said anything else?

FRANCES. No.

SRINIVAS. Nothing more about this baby business?

FRANCES. No. Jane and Mark have got a son.

SRINIVAS. Really?

FRANCES. Yes. He's five, that's right, isn't it Mark?

MARK. What have you done to my wife?

SRINIVAS. I beg your pardon?

MARK. I said, what have you done to my wife?

SRINIVAS. 'Done to her'?

MARK (*indicating* FRANCES). She said she was with you. Weeks ago.

SRINIVAS. Well, I assume she was with you weeks before that. So what did you 'do' to her?

MARK. Did you bring her here?

SRINIVAS. What do you mean?

MARK. To India? Did you bring her to India?

SRINIVAS. Oh, I see. You think I lured her here, like some sinister Svengali. Or was it white-slavery you had in mind?

MARK. So, where does she know you from? Well? You must have met her somewhere!

SRINIVAS. Certainly not in England. I haven't been in England since I left Oxford.

MARK. So where did you meet her?

SRINIVAS. You're not a policeman are you? By any chance?
In real life? I met her at Chennnai Central.

FRANCES. The railway station.

SRINIVAS. I run a shelter for street kids. We try to intercept
children coming in from the villages. The Kanyakumari
express had just come in and I saw her on the platform. She
had made the rather foolish mistake of giving a fifty rupee
note to a beggar. She was being mobbed. I went and rescued
her, threw the crowd some coins. She seemed nervous.
Disturbed.

MARK. Disturbed?

SRINIVAS. Yes. So I took her for a cup of tea in the station
café.

MARK. And then what?

SRINIVAS. We shared a masala bun, I think.

MARK (*indicating* FRANCES). She said she worked for you.

SRINIVAS. She worked for the charity. She stayed at the
shelter, helped with the children. It was what she wanted
to do.

MARK. And you never wondered who she was? I mean, you
never asked her where she'd come from? You never thought
of ringing anyone?

SRINIVAS. She was very reluctant to speak about herself.
And I don't share your taste for interrogation. But we did
talk a great deal about other things. About life. About God.
Your wife has an extremely original mind; an extraordinary
perspective on the world.

MARK. You don't need to tell me about my wife. I know my
wife.

SRINIVAS. I don't think you know her very well at all.

MARK. You what?

FRANCES. Vas . . .

SRINIVAS. If you knew her well, you wouldn't be surprised that she had come here. You wouldn't be looking for a scapegoat, when the reasons she left quite clearly lie within herself.

For a moment it seems that MARK *is going to attack* SRINIVAS. *But at that moment,* JANE *enters.*

FRANCES *sees her first.*

FRANCES. Mark.

MARK *and* SRINIVAS *follow* FRANCES*'s gaze. They see* JANE. MARK *pales, as though he has seen a ghost.*

JANE *is in her late twenties. She has short, cropped hair. She is wearing a vest and a sarong. She is holding a white plastic carrier bag, that seems neither heavy or full. But it is not empty. When she finally speaks, she has a strong regional accent (from somewhere that places her well away from London).*

She stares at MARK.

SRINIVAS *is smiling.*

SRINIVAS. Jane.

But FRANCES *takes his arm.*

FRANCES. Come on.

He looks at FRANCES *almost angrily for a moment.*

(*To* MARK *and* JANE.) We'll be in the garden.

SRINIVAS *walks out quickly.* FRANCES *follows.*

JANE *and* MARK *continue to stare at each other. The silence lasts several moments.*

MARK. You've cut your hair.

Pause.

JANE. I had lice.

Pause.

MARK. It suits you.

JANE. You don't like me with short hair.

MARK. I like you any way.

Pause.

Jesus, Jane . . .

It hangs on the air, filling the silence. After a moment, JANE crosses to him and hugs him, quite formally. The bag hangs down over his back. He receives the hug, unsure of it, of her. She lets him go. She glances at his luggage by the door.

JANE. Have you brought Joe?

MARK. I've brought you some stuff. T-shirts and that.
I thought you might need them.

JANE. Thanks.

MARK. A jumper. Not a woolly one. That one you said can go in the wash. A summer jumper.

Pause.

JANE. Have you brought Joe?

Pause.

MARK. What?

Pause.

Have I brought Joe? Is that what you said?

JANE. Yes.

MARK. Have I brought Joe?

JANE. Yes.

MARK. Is that what you thought I'd do? Bring him halfway round the world to see some woman who might not even be his mother?

JANE *can't answer.*

Make him take malaria pills? Make him sit on a plane for hours and hours? No, I haven't brought him. Funnily enough. He's with my mum. He's been with my mum a lot lately.

Do you know how old my mum is? She's sixty-five years old. She shouldn't be looking after a five-year-old: taking him to school, collecting him from school, giving him his tea. She shouldn't be putting him to bed, bathing him, bathing him while dad gets left with a t.v dinner!

Pause.

Well? Aren't you going to say something?

Pause.

What, that's it is it? You're just going to stand there? Have you any idea what you've done to us? What you've done to Joe?

JANE. Is he all right?

MARK. No! No, he's not all right! He's lost his mum, hasn't he? He doesn't understand any of this. He thinks it's his fault. And what am I supposed to say? Because I don't understand it either. Well?

Pause.

I don't believe this.

Pause.

What's going on, Jane?

Pause.

What's going on?

JANE *cannot speak. She can't even look at him. She is trembling slightly.*

I've had it with this. I've really had it with this. I tell you, I'd rather have found you dead, I'd rather be identifying your body in some morgue, in some mortuary than have you standing there like this. Just standing there like nothing's happened. Are you seeing someone else?

JANE *looks at him, shocked.*

Him is it? Jungle-book boy?

JANE *stares at him, barely able to answer.*

JANE. No.

MARK. Are you pregnant? Is that what this is?

JANE. Pregnant?

MARK. Were you pregnant? Because that's what she thought. She didn't say it but she thought it. You were pregnant and you had an abortion.

JANE. No.

MARK. Because if you did that, if you got rid of our baby because you can't be bothered to bring up another kid . . .

JANE. I wasn't pregnant.

MARK. That would have been a brother or sister for Joe . . .

JANE. I wasn't pregnant.

MARK. Well, what's this about a baby then? A baby in a bag? (*He points to the carrier bag.*) What's that then?

JANE reacts physically to this, as though she has been stung.

Well?

JANE. Don't.

MARK. Don't ? Don't? Don't what? Don't what? You stupid, stupid, selfish cow!

Silence. MARK has shocked himself. He feels distraught. He sits down, tries to control himself.

JANE is still trembling.

JANE (*quietly*). I'm sorry.

Pause.

MARK. Sorry? Sorry's what you say when you forget to put the rubbish out on a bin-day. What is it you say to Joe? Sorry's all very well but you have to mean it.

JANE. I do mean it.

Pause.

MARK. Seven weeks.

Pause.

Do you know what I thought? I thought you'd been drugged
or kidnapped or something. I just didn't want to think that
you'd done it on purpose. Sometimes I'd be watching telly
late at night and I'd think, God, what am I doing? What am
I doing sitting here? She could be out there, she could be
out there crying for me, screaming for me. I thought
someone had come round and put something in your tea or
something. Made you pack your things, tidy everything . . .
I saw this film once about a man who kidnapped women off
the streets – just ordinary women, secretaries going to work,
Mums, and he put them in this room and he chained them
up and he starved them to death. He didn't touch them or
speak to them. He just starved them to death. And he would
come back every day and watch them; photograph them,
listen to them pleading . . .

He trails off. Pause.

That's how you've been, in my head. In my dreams.

Silence. JANE *moves towards him. She sits down close to
him.*

Is there someone else? I just want to know, all right? I just
want you to tell me so I know.

Long pause.

JANE. When Joe was born . . .

Pause.

MARK. Yes?

Pause.

What?

JANE. When Joe was born, when I was in hospital, they gave
me a box, full of things. Free things for new babies.
Nappies. Baby food. Teething gel.

Pause.

MARK. So?

Pause.

JANE. At the bottom of the box there was an envelope. It had red writing on the front. It said, 'What does a new mother in India get for her baby?' And I opened it up and it said, 'Nothing'.

Pause.

Do you remember it?

MARK. No.

JANE. I kept it by the bed.

Pause.

I get all these letters from charities. Asking me for money. They send things to me because I'm a mother and they know that I watch every spoonful of food that goes into my child's mouth and that I love to watch him chewing and swallowing and opening his mouth for more. I know all these things now. And when you know . . .

Pause.

MARK. What?

JANE. I know there's a disease in Africa called The Grazer, that eats through the faces of children. It leaves holes where their noses and mouths would have been. And the children can't fight it because they're too weak and there isn't any money to buy the medicine to stop it. I know about a village not far from here where they can't afford to bring up girls, they can't afford to pay their dowries. So when a baby girl's born they take her from her mother and press her face into a sack of grain until she's dead. And there's Joe: and we worry that he might not wake up one morning and that's real. But then we worry that he didn't walk as early as the baby down the road and that sometimes he stutters when he's searching for a word and what if he minds that his new video is not a Disney one but a cheap thing we picked up on a market stall and should we put a prize in every layer of pass-the-parcel or just one prize at the end and in that case will there be a riot? I know about the orphans in Albania who pace the bars of their cots like animals in bad zoos and the little girls in Ghana who want to be doctors but get married off when they're twelve and raped and treated like slaves, and the babies in South Africa who get thrown into bins because they've got Aids. And there's Joe. There's Joe. And we worry that he might run into the road one day and that's real. But then we worry that he won't learn to read as quickly as he should and he won't be clever enough and pass exams and go to college and get better jobs than we've had and make more money so that he can have a bigger house and a bigger car and more things.

Pause. She looks at MARK, *who is staring at her, bewildered.*

There was a woman in the shanty-town, sitting on the ground outside her hut, with a baby pressed to her breast. It was so thin, this baby. A big head, with arms and legs dangling, like paper. And the woman was thin too. And her breast was nothing. And it was hopeless. With the flies all around them. Hopeless. And I waited. And when it was dark I put everything I had inside an envelope – my money, my passport, my rings and . . . and . . .

She stops. She cannot go on. Her brain jams. Panic sets in.

MARK. And what? And what? You gave her your stuff? Did you? Jane?

JANE *is on her feet now. She has grabbed the bag and is heading for the door.* MARK *intercepts her.*

No, you don't.

JANE. Let me go . . .

MARK. Are you saying . . . Are you saying that you came here to . . . What? To help? Is that what all this is? You . . .

JANE. I have to go . . .

MARK. You puts us through all this because you got a few letters from Oxfam? Jesus Christ Almighty! I'm sorry but this is unbelievable! This is laughable! This is laughable!

JANE. I have to go.

MARK. You've torn our whole family apart because you've got a bleeding heart? What were you going to do? Come and find Mother Teresa? Ask her if she needs a hand?

She stops still.

JANE. Mother Teresa? Mother Teresa is dead.

MARK. So, what, you were going to be the new one were you? Mother Jane of Kensal Rise? This is laughable. You can't even sit on the same tube as a stinky bloke. You're the first one to get off and change carriages. You're worse than me! If you really wanted to help, why didn't you . . . I don't know . . . go down the old folks home or something, play a few rounds of bingo with them, but no! You've got to go halfway round the world, you've got to go all the way to India, all the way to India! Well, that's it. I've had enough. You're coming home. Get your stuff.

JANE. What?

MARK. I've had enough. We'll sort out your passport, we'll go to the airport. We'll sit there until there's a flight and we'll get on it. (*Pointing to the bag.*) And you can give me that as well.

JANE. No.

MARK. Just give it to me, Jane!

JANE moves away.

Just give it to me!

He makes a grab for the bag.

JANE (*shouting*). Leave it!

MARK. What is it? One you didn't rescue? One you couldn't save?

He grabs her and tries to get the bag off her. FRANCES *and* SRINIVAS *run in.*

SRINIVAS. Leave her!

MARK turns on him.

FRANCES. Stop it, Mark!

MARK. She's coming home!

JANE has retreated. She is covering her ears with her hands and murmuring to herself continuously –

JANE. Medam, Medam . . . Medam, Medam . . .

SRINIVAS. She doesn't want to.

MARK. She's coming home with me!

JANE. Medam, Medam . . . Medam, Medam . . .

FRANCES. This isn't helping!

SRINIVAS. Don't listen to him, Jane . . .

MARK. You shut it, and leave her alone!

SRINIVAS. You leave her alone!

FRANCES. Stop it!

JANE (*growing louder*). Medam, Medam . . . Medam, Medam . . . I've got nothing. I've got nothing. I've got nothing. I've got nothing!

She runs out towards the garden, leaving the others standing. MARK is shocked, appalled. FRANCES looks accusingly at SRINIVAS.

Scene Two

The garden. Ferocious sunlight. The chatter of birds. A well-worn garden table and chairs sit under the shade of a vine-covered terrace.

Nearby, JANE is crouching on the ground, bent double over the carrier-bag which she clutches to her stomach. Her face is hidden. She is very still.

SRINIVAS *is heard calling.*

SRINIVAS. Jane!

A moment later he enters.

Jane!

He sees her and stops.

Jane.

She turns even further away from him. He knows that he shouldn't approach her.

He sits down at the table. He takes papers and tobacco from his pocket and rolls a cigarette. Long pause.

Did he hurt you?

She doesn't reply.

I can't believe you're married to a man like that. I imagined all sorts of things for you, but not him. I suppose you're going to tell me that he's all right really, once you get to know him. I've got several friends with appalling husbands; at least most of their marriages were arranged. I can't believe you actually chose him.

Pause.

JANE (*quietly*). He would never hurt me. He just holds me too tightly sometimes.

SRINIVAS. I'm supposed to be impressed by that, am I? Come into the shade. You're burning your skin.

She doesn't move.

I have to go the shelter for a few hours. I'll be back this evening. I need you to promise me you'll still be here.

Silence

All right, don't promise. I don't know what I'm doing, I never ask for promises. Just be here. No matter what he says, you don't have to go back with him. You don't have to go anywhere.

Pause.

Jane?

Silence. He takes a piece of folded paper out of his pocket and holds it out to her.

I've got something for you.

She looks at the paper. After a moment, she crosses to the table. She sits on a chair and puts the bag down next to it. She takes the paper from him and unfolds it slowly. It is a child's drawing.

It's from Keya.

She smiles.

That's you. Apparently. And that's her, with all the plaits you did for her. They've proved very popular, those plaits. We've had a steady stream of girls at the door, asking for the same style. You've started a trend.

JANE. It's great.

SRINIVAS. I told her I'd give it to you.

JANE is still smiling, remembering the shelter.

JANE. How's Velu?

SRINIVAS. Your little Velu is fine. I found those boys and paid off his debt. He's rag-picking again. He's getting pretty nifty at it.

JANE. He shouldn't have to do it.

SRINIVAS. It's a living. At least we know where to find him. At least we can clean him up every few weeks.

She nods.

And I don't know what you said to Ardu, but he's started turning up at school. I don't think they really want him there, he's so disruptive, but . . .

JANE. He's clever.

SRINIVAS. Yes.

Pause.

So . . . when are you coming back?

Pause.

I want you to come back, Jane. I want you to go on working with me.

JANE. I can't.

SRINIVAS. Why? Why not? You said it felt right, being with us. You said you had found where you were meant to be. Or have you changed your mind now?

JANE (*definitely*). No.

Pause. They look at each other intensely for a moment, then she looks away again.

SRINIVAS. Jane, India does strange things to people. It's a cliché, but it's true. It can leave your soul completely exposed. And yours is such a large soul. Such a beautiful soul. Look at me. Please.

She does so.

I don't know what happened after you left. I don't even know why you left.

She looks down.

Frances told me about how she found you. About you crying. About that. (*He indicates the bag.*) Whatever happened, whatever is troubling you, we can work through it. We can make sense of it. Just come back with me.

JANE (*instantly*). I can't. I can't come back with you.

SRINIVAS. I know you have a son. Bring him here. He can live with us at the shelter.

Pause.

JANE. Bring him here?

SRINIVAS. Yes. Why not?

JANE. He's five.

SRINIVAS. So? Think how we could expand his horizons. We'll teach him to meditate. We'll teach him yoga. We'll make a great thinker of him.

JANE *smiles suddenly.*

What? I'm serious.

JANE. I know. I know you are.

SRINIVAS. He'll learn more here in a week than he would in a year of school and . . . what is it? *Teletubbies.*

She laughs.

Jane.

He leans towards her and kisses her on the mouth. The kiss goes on for some time.

FRANCES *enters. She sees them and stops still. A look of dismay passes across her face. She leaves, unseen.*

JANE *stops the kiss and moves away from the table. She stares at him, not angrily but questioningly. He returns her gaze with steady, unblinking eyes.*

Scene Three

The living room. MARK *is sitting with his head in his hands.*

FRANCES *enters from the garden. She walks quickly to a sideboard and takes out a bottle of brandy.*

MARK. Is she all right?

FRANCES. Yes. Well, she's still here anyway.

She pours a drink.

Would you like a drink?

MARK. No thanks . . .

FRANCES. I mean a drink drink.

MARK *looks at the the brandy.*

MARK. All right. Thanks.

She pours another and takes it to him, before going back to her own, which she drinks quickly.

They are silent for a few moments. Frances grows calmer. She looks at Mark. He is still very shocked. Lost.

FRANCES. You know, a lot of people come to India to help. For a short time. It's not as rare as you might think. People used to go to Mother Teresa all the time and ask what they could do. All kinds of people; opera singers, teachers. I even met an estate agent once who had come to do his bit.

Pause.

MARK. She should have told me.

FRANCES. Yes.

MARK. She said it started after Joe was born. All these charities started sending her stuff. It's sick: picking on people when they're feeling . . .

He trails off.

FRANCES. I suppose the charities would say they have no choice: they have to get the money off people any way they . . .

MARK. It all makes sense now. I went through our bank statements after she'd gone. I checked them properly. There was all this money going out to charities: five pounds here, ten pounds there. Standing orders. I thought she'd just been caught out a few times. You know? Nobbled by those people who stand in the street with arm bands and clip boards. Do you know, they get paid, those people who stand on the street? They're not doing it out of the goodness of their hearts. It's not like your old lady shaking a tin. They get paid. They get trained in trapping people, taking people for mugs. Well, it's all going to stop when I get back. I'm going to cancel them. All of them. I'm going to ring them all and tell them to stop sending stuff. I'm going to tell them what they've done to her.

Pause.

I'm going to take her down the doctors. Get her sorted out. Get her some pills or something.

FRANCES. Pills may not be the answer, Mark.

MARK (*sharply*). If she needs them, she needs them.

SRINIVAS *enters. He goes straight to where he left his things and starts gathering them together.*

SRINIVAS. I've got to go. I'll come back this evening.

MARK. Don't bother.

SRINIVAS (*to* FRANCES). Will you call me, if anything happens?

He looks at her for the first time since entering the room. She hesitates for a moment before answering, as though she would like to say something else. But his gaze demands a straight-forward answer.

FRANCES. Yes.

MARK (*to* SRINIVAS). You know, you're the problem here: people like you, getting her all wound up about poor kids and diseases. She came because of you lot.

SRINIVAS. Really?

MARK. Why don't you just stay away from her? Let her get on with her life?

FRANCES. I think you should go, Vas.

SRINIVAS. Some people would be proud of that. Some people would say it took a great deal of courage to come here.

MARK. She wasn't thinking straight, that's all. Everything just got on top of her.

SRINIVAS. She was thinking straight enough to apply for a visa. She must have been planning to come for several days before she left.

This hits home, but MARK *won't admit it* –

MARK. Just stay away from her, all right?

SRINIVAS. Don't you believe in charity, Mark?

MARK. Just stay away from her!

SRINIVAS. No, really. I'm interested. Don't you believe in charity?

FRANCES (*under her breath*). For God's sake.

MARK. I believe in family. That's what I believe in. I'll give my tenner at Christmas just like anyone, but I believe in family. Before anything else. You look after your own. And she's got a family. She's got me and Joe. And she should be looking after us.

SRINIVAS. And everyone else can just go hang themselves?

MARK. Yes. That's right. That's right. If we all sat around feeling sorry for everyone else, nothing would ever get done, would it? I mean, some of us have just got to get on with our lives. Make a living. It's like at Joe's school, there are all these kids, refugees, who can't even speak English and they hold the others back. They stop the others learning anything because the teacher's always with them, teaching them 'hello' and 'goodbye' and 'where's the toilet?' It's luck, isn't it, where you're born, who you're born to? And if you want to change it, it's up to you. You have to get on and do it. There are always going to be some people better off than other people. There are rich countries and poor countries. It's just luck. My mum's always saying, aren't we lucky to be English? You can't make everyone the same. That's what the Russians tried to do and look where it got them.

Pause.

SRINIVAS. You've obviously given this a great deal of thought . . .

MARK. Yes. Yes, I have.

SRINIVAS. And you don't think that perhaps it suits the richer countries to keep some of the other countries poor? In order to exploit them? To use them as a source of cheap labour? A source of . . .

MARK (*speaking over the top of him*). It's the other way round.

SRINIVAS. . . . cheap resources?

MARK. It's the other way round. You lot exploit us. You come over, you take our jobs, you use our health service, our social . . .

SRINIVAS. Really?

MARK. Yes, really. Where did you say you went to university?

SRINIVAS. Oxford.

MARK. Oh! Oxford, was it?

SRINIVAS. But I did my original degree in Madras . . .

MARK. You know, it's so crowded in London now, we can't even buy a house. There's no way we can move from a flat to a house because the prices have gone through the roof because there are too many people wanting property. Because there are a load of people in London who shouldn't even be there.

SRINIVAS. And you think they should just go back where they came from?

MARK. Yes. That's exactly what I think. And so do most people if they're being honest. Everyone should just stay in their own countries. Sort out their own problems. It would make life a lot easier.

Pause. SRINIVAS *turns away and begins picking up his things.*

SRINIVAS. What a fascist you are.

MARK. I'm no fascist.

SRINIVAS. You're a fascist and a racist.

MARK. No I'm not.

SRINIVAS. Pathetic.

MARK. There are black blokes on my football team.

SRINIVAS. Truly pathetic.

MARK. I play football with black blokes.

SRINIVAS. Why don't you just gas all the immigrants and have done?

MARK. Oh, that's right, that's right. It's so easy, isn't it? Call someone a racist and they're supposed to just shut up. It's got so you can't be honest any more. Because the Jews died no-one's allowed to talk a bit of common sense.

SRINIVAS (*with mock interest*). Oh, I see.

MARK. It doesn't work, all these people going into other people's countries. I mean, people will put up with it for so long, they'll keep quiet for so long, but then it'll take just one thing, one big . . . what's it . . . recession, one big year of unemployment and that'll be it – there'll be a backlash. And I don't just mean riots, I mean a civil war.

SRINIVAS (*smiling*). My God, you people are so small-minded.

MARK. I'm just telling it how it is.

SRINIVAS. The whole world revolves around you.

MARK. I'm just telling it how it is.

SRINIVAS. And you wonder why September the eleventh happened.

SRINIVAS. And you wonder why September the eleventh happened.

MARK. I'm just . . . September the eleventh, oh yeah, I bet you loved that, didn't you? I bet you were out there dancing on the streets.

SRINIVAS. No I wasn't, as it happens.

MARK. Yeah, right.

SRINIVAS. But I did allow myself a smile.

MARK. A smile?

SRINIVAS. Yes, for just one moment, I smiled. Not because I believe in what they did . . .

MARK. You smiled?

SRINIVAS. I smiled at the audacity of the gesture. You know, very soon the whole way the world . . .

MARK. I think that's disgusting.

SRINIVAS. . . . works is going to change. The . . .

MARK. I think that's disgusting that you smiled.

SRINIVAS. . . . debts are going to be wiped out and the markets are going to be opened up and countries like yours are going to . . .

MARK. People threw themselves out of windows!

SRINIVAS. . . . have to start paying the true price for . . .

MARK. Nothing anyone's ever done to you is as bad as that.

SRINIVAS. . . . what you use. The whole world is going to open up and no-one is going to want to come to your country anymore.

MARK. Good! Good! About time!

SRINIVAS. And your country will become sick, hopelessly, terminally sick, until it finally implodes under its own obese, corrupted weight!

MARK. Oh, I'm really scared.

SRINIVAS. Then perhaps you'll be the bottom of the heap. Perhaps it will be your turn to watch your infants die.

MARK. I'm really scared!

SRINIVAS. You should be. It's not that far away.

MARK. I'm really scared, I'm really scared!

SRINIVAS *stops and stares at him, with a mixture of amusement and disdain.* FRANCES *is staring at him too.* MARK *realises that, in a way, he seems just that – really scared.*

SRINIVAS *picks up his things and leaves. His footsteps can be heard along the hall and then the sound of the front door opening and closing.*

MARK *suddenly hurls his glass at the doorway. It hits the frame and shatters.*

FRANCES *does not move. Silence.* MARK *sits down suddenly. He takes a scrap of tissue from his pocket and wipes his face, but it disintegrates into a useless mess.*

God. God!

He throws it off his hand. Pause.

I'm sorry.

FRANCES. It's all right.

MARK. It's not all right. It's not all right. I'm not normally like this.

FRANCES. No.

MARK. I'm not.

FRANCES. I know.

MARK *gets up and moves towards where the glass is.*

Leave it, Mark.

MARK. No, I'll just . . .

FRANCES. Leave it. Please. I want you to go and have a lie down. I've cleared some space in my studio. There's a sofa-cum-bed sort of thing. And there's a shower. Only hand-held, but it does work.

MARK. Right.

He hesitates. FRANCES *picks up his bag. He is still standing, staring at the ground.*

FRANCES. Come on.

He looks up at her and nods. He follows her out.

After a few moments, JANE *enters and stops. She takes in the empty room, the broken glass on the floor.*

FRANCES *enters and sees her. She doesn't smile, or engage with her. She crosses to where the glass is and begins to pick up the pieces.*

JANE. What happened?

FRANCES. Nothing. A difference of opinion, that's all.

JANE. He hasn't gone has he?

FRANCES (*pointedly*). Which one?

Pause.

JANE. Mark.

FRANCES. No. He's upstairs.

Pause. FRANCES *carries on picking up the glass.* JANE *starts across to the door to the stairs.*

I'd leave him for a little while.

JANE *stops.*

This must be very difficult for him. He must be jet-lagged on top of everything else.

JANE. Yes.

Pause. JANE *goes to help* FRANCES *with the glass.*

FRANCES. Leave it, it's all right.

JANE *continues.*

It's easier if I do it myself.

JANE *stops. She watches* FRANCES *for a moment.*

JANE. Frances?

FRANCES. Yes?

JANE. I'm sorry.

FRANCES. What for?

JANE. For bringing all this . . . trouble. For ruining your peace.

FRANCES. Peace? Is that what you think I have?

Pause.

JANE. I'm really grateful to you. For helping me.

FRANCES. You needn't be.

JANE. For finding me.

FRANCES. It was Vas who told me to look out for you.

JANE. But you didn't have to bring me here. You knew it would help me. And it has.

FRANCES finishes with the glass and sits back. She looks at JANE.

FRANCES. I'm glad.

She smiles at her. JANE sits down opposite her, placing the carrier-bag beside her. Silence. FRANCES is considering her.

My husband used to shout a lot too. It can be quite hard.

JANE. Yes.

FRANCES. If you're not a shouting sort of person.

Pause.

I think Mark's shouting is different though. It seems to me that Mark shouts when he's feeling . . . confused, or threatened, I suppose. Richard just shouted because he thought he was better than everyone else. Everyone else was never quite up to scratch. And he was terribly good with words. He could devastate people with his words. Waiters mostly.

Pause.

Mark tells me you have a son.

JANE. Yes.

FRANCES. Joe, isn't it?

JANE. Yes.

FRANCES. That's lovely. I've got boys. Well, they're men now. My eldest is thirty-one.

Pause.

JANE. Where are they?

FRANCES. London. The younger one's still with his father. He's still studying, so I suppose it makes sense. Financially.

Pause.

FRANCES. And David's got a flat.

JANE. Do they ever come here?

FRANCES. No. I expect they will. Eventually.

Pause. JANE *is staring at her, scrutinising her.*

I miss them. Of course. I ring them sometimes but it's hard to catch them in. Quite right too.

Pause.

JANE. When I first came here, I woke up every morning with Joe's face filling my head; this big, blonde face, like a full moon. But then I kind of . . . put him away. I didn't stop caring for him. But he's just a different part of me. That I'm not living.

MARK *has entered silently. He is listening.*

I sometimes think . . .

She trails off.

FRANCES. Go on.

JANE. I sometimes think that we exaggerate our feelings for our kids. We use them as an excuse not to live properly. Not to find out what it's all about. We've got them and they need us so that's all right. What is it Vas says? People like to own things, even other people, because it makes us feel safe; it makes us matter.

MARK. I haven't got a towel.

FRANCES *stands in surprise.* JANE *looks at him. He stares back at her. There are tears in his eyes.*

FRANCES. Oh yes, I'm sorry. I forgot about that. Let me get you one.

MARK (*to* JANE). Go on. Go on. It's very interesting, hearing how you don't love your own kid.

Pause.

JANE. That's . . .

MARK. What kind of mother are you? Well, I can answer that, can't I? A useless one. A bad one.

FRANCES. Mark . . .

MARK. I mean, what kind of mother just ups and leaves her child without telling him where she's going, without telling him when she'll be back? (*To* FRANCES.) Would you have done that? Just left your kids when they were Joe's age?

FRANCES *hesitates.*

FRANCES. No, but . . .

MARK. No normal mother would.

FRANCES. But perhaps I would have done . . . if I had felt desperate enough.

MARK. You know, you always used to make me think that I was bad with Joe. You used to make me think that I was getting it wrong all the time, that I couldn't deal with him. But I tell you what, we've been fine since you left. We've been great. And you're the one who can't deal with him. I know that now. You're the one who can't cope.

Pause.

I mean, this is what this is all about, isn't it? You can't cope so you ran away. You can't cope with Joe, you can't cope with any of it.

Pause.

JANE. Perhaps I am a bad mother. I don't know . . . if there are bad mothers and good mothers.

MARK. You are a bad mother. No 'perhaps', you are a bad mother.

JANE. I don't remember coming here. I remember standing over the bathroom sink, crying like I was vomiting. I can remember turning to you and feeling like you were on a TV. screen, and the sound was down. And then suddenly

you were right in front of my face, panicking, spitting
all this fear, shouting that the world was going to get in
through the cracks in the walls and that it would finish us
and it would finish Joe and there would be nothing left. And
I'd watch you leaving for work every day and I'd know that
you had no hope of yourself, no hope except that Joe would
grow up one day and make it all better. I don't remember
coming here. But I know that I had to come. I had to get
back to . . . something simple. I just knew that . . . that I had
to get down on my knees and help someone who couldn't
help themselves. Help someone to get through the night.
Help someone not to die.

Long pause.

MARK. Fine. Fine. I'll tell you what then, Jane, you just stay
here. Just don't come back, all right? Because you're sick.
You're sick. So you just stay here and do your crawling
around or whatever it is you have to do, because we don't
need you. All right? We don't need you anywhere near us.
So just stay away, all right? Just stay away from us.

*He leaves the room and goes back upstairs. FRANCES
looks at JANE for a moment and then goes after him. JANE
is left, alone.*

ACT TWO

Scene One

The garden. Late afternoon. The heat is less intense. JANE is sitting at the table, with the carrier bag on the ground beside her chair. FRANCES is sitting at the opposite side of the table. She is sketching JANE. The brandy bottle is on the table, and two glasses.

They have been there for some time.

FRANCES. We met at a party. I was at Art College and he'd just come down from Cambridge. Where he'd made his mark, of course. Someone pointed him out across the room and whispered something about 'A first class brain'. People were always saying that about him. I hate that, don't you? That idea that some people have better brains than others. Surely it's just that some parts of people's brains are better developed than other parts, or that some people are taught to use their brains properly. I don't know, perhaps that's wishful thinking.

She stops and rubs out some of the drawing.

I can't get your arms right at all.

Pause.

Anyway, I wandered out to look at the river – the party was near the Embankment. It was a beautiful evening. The river was all lit up. It was magical. And after a minute, I realised there was someone beside me. It was Richard. He'd followed me out. We stood for a while, watching the water. We shared a cigarette. And then he started talking and I thought, goodness, I could listen to you for the rest of my life.

She starts drawing again.

You're wonderfully still.

Pause.

We just got married. Almost straight away. Snuck off to a registry office. No photos. No parents. I didn't even finish my course. My friends thought I was mad. It was all women's lib at the time. Getting married was like selling your soul. But I just wanted to live with Richard, in a lovely house, and have lovely babies. And have them while I was still young. I didn't want to be an old mum. Do you remember that advert, for some sort of face cream, where there's a mother and a sort of twenty-year-old daughter and a man in a shop can't tell which one is which? Well . . . I think that had something to do with it.

She smiles. She stops drawing and takes a drink.

Only, I didn't have a daughter. I had two hulking great boys. But I loved being a mother. I loved it. All those walks in the park, taking them to prep school, meeting my friends, buying their clothes, baking, little aprons for painting. It was bliss. (*Pause.*) It was the best bit. The best bit of my life. And it's over so quickly.

She looks at JANE, *who is looking down, watches her for a few moments. Then she starts drawing again.*

How did you meet Mark?

Pause. It is hard for JANE *to answer this direct question.*

JANE. I met him in a café, where I was working. I'd just moved to London. I didn't know anyone. Mark used to come in with his mates. Most days. He used to smile at me. He used to put everything on the tray when they'd finished – plates and serviettes and everything, and bring it back to the counter for me. 'Save your legs.'

Pause. FRANCES *has stopped drawing.*

FRANCES. That was kind.

Pause.

He obviously loves you. A lot.

Pause.

JANE. Vas says there's no such thing as kindness. He says every act of kindness is a demand for something back.

FRANCES. Does he?

Pause.

Jane . . .

JANE. What happened? To you and your husband?

FRANCES. What happened? Oh, I don't really know. Well, I do. The usual sort of thing, I suppose. I think he just lost interest in me. It's as simple as that.

JANE. That's not simple.

FRANCES. Isn't it? I don't know. There were all these girls at work. Girls with ideas of their own who could give him a run for his money. I don't know. He needs to feel that he's running with the hounds. He had married this . . . dare I say, beautiful, girl; a little unconventional, wanted to be an artist, wanted to take London by storm, and there I was, this middle-aged woman, nagging him about holiday dates, moaning on about the au-pairs.

She half-smiles at JANE. *She refills her glass.*

Things really fell apart once the boys left school. Even then, we carried on for a while. Years. It's amazing, isn't it, our capacity for 'carrying on'? We can walk around with holes the size of cannonballs in the centre of our stomachs and still smile. Why aren't people crying in the streets? I often think that? There's so much unhappiness around and yet I never see anyone crying in the street. Except you.

Long pause. They look at each other. A moment of real contact. Recognition.

JANE. Why did you leave?

Pause.

FRANCES. He started an affair, a serious one. And I'd . . .

She trails off. She seems to blush at the thought of something. Pause.

We had stopped wanting each other. Physically. I didn't want him anywhere near me. I used to lie at the very edge of the bed every night, terrified that we might touch each other, accidentally. I didn't even want to feel the heat coming off his body. Imagine that: being so appalled by another person's warmth.

Pause.

The morning of the day I left, he got up before me. He had to go to a meeting. And as he got out of bed, the sheet and blankets caught around his leg and they fell onto the floor. But he didn't stop and pick them up, cover me up again, he just left them and put on his dressing-gown. And I lay there, looking faintly ridiculous, I suppose, with my nightie tucked up around my legs, and I thought, if someone were to take a photograph of this now, it would look like a double negative – you know, two pictures taken over the top of each other, and it was an accident that we were in the same picture at all; there was really no relationship between us, we didn't belong in the same space, or the same time even.

Pause. She is lost in thought, memory, pain. She is visibly shaken.

So I packed my things.

Pause.

JANE. That was brave.

FRANCES. No. No, it wasn't brave. It was the right thing to do, but it wasn't brave. Jane, can I give you some advice? It's not something I normally do, give advice, but . . . I just think it would be such a shame if . . . if you decided about things, I mean if you decided about anything because of . . .

SRINIVAS *enters.* FRANCES *stops speaking, abruptly and looks away. He crosses to them and stops. He stares at* JANE *with smiling, triumphant eyes.*

SRINIVAS. You're still here.

JANE. Yes.

FRANCES (*suddenly*). No, no, Vas, she isn't. That's just a mirage. She left. Hours ago. Sorry.

SRINIVAS *looks at* FRANCES *calmly, coldly, taking in her mood. He puts his jacket over the back of a chair and sits down.*

SRINIVAS. Am I interrupting something?

FRANCES. Would it matter if you were?

Pause.

SRINIVAS. So, where is he?

FRANCES. If you mean Mark, Mark has gone to the village. To phone home.

JANE. Should he have been back by now?

FRANCES. No, not necessarily. The man who runs the phone isn't there sometimes. Sometimes you have to wait for a line.

SRINIVAS. Was he walking? I'm surprised I didn't pass him.

FRANCES. No. He took the old bicycle from the shed.

SRINIVAS (*smiling wryly*). Now that I would like to have seen.

FRANCES. What?

SRINIVAS. Him on a bicycle. I can't quite imagine it somehow – well, actually I can – sweating his way along the road, cursing as he wobbles up the hill.

FRANCES. Has it ever occurred to you, Vas, that people aren't actually the way you see them? That your view of things is subjective, just as everyone's is? That you have reasons for seeing things the way you do? Has that ever occurred to you?

Pause.

SRINIVAS. I only said that he must look funny on a bicycle.

FRANCES. Well he didn't. He looked perfectly at home on a bicycle.

Pause. SRINIVAS *looks at* JANE. *He wants to talk to her.* FRANCES *is watching him. She isn't going to move.*

SRINIVAS. Can I have a drink? Or do you need the whole bottle?

FRANCES. Of course you can have a drink.

SRINIVAS. Thank you. I need a glass.

FRANCES. Well go and get one then. You know where they are.

Pause. After a moment, SRINIVAS *reaches for* JANE's *glass. He pulls it towards him.*

SRINIVAS (*to* JANE). You don't mind, do you?

JANE (*hesitant*). No.

He fills it. He drinks and puts it down. He looks at FRANCES.

SRINIVAS. We're sharing.

FRANCES *gets up from the table and turns away. She gazes out over the garden. Pause.*

I didn't mean to stop you drawing, Frances.

Silence.

JANE. Those pink flowers are about to come out. On the tree.

SRINIVAS. Yes. Magnolia.

JANE. I think this is the best garden I've ever been in.

SRINIVAS. Yes. It's wonderful.

JANE. It's like those blue and white pictures you see on plates. I think it's the way the trees hang down like that. And the water running down the rocks.

SRINIVAS. You're right. That's exactly what it's like. Frances used to play in this garden when she was a child. Did she tell you?

JANE. No.

SRINIVAS. This house belonged to my grandparents. Frances's father and my grandfather were friends. So little Frances used to be brought here, to play with my mother. That's right, isn't it, Frances?

Pause.

FRANCES. Yes. Yes, that's right.

She returns to the table.

Vas's mother and I were best friends for a time. We're about the same age. Vas likes to hear me say that for some reason.

SRINIVAS. No, I just think it's a charming story, that's all.

FRANCES (*harshly*). I loved coming here. It was much cooler here than in the city. I'd have come every day if I could. It was like paradise. We would play together, for hours and hours. Left all to ourselves. We had a tree-house in the big tree at the end there. You can still see part of the ladder in the branches. Charming, isn't it?

JANE *doesn't reply.*

We stayed in touch, even after I left India. Wrote to each other. Then when we were older, we made visits; introduced our families. So you see, when I first met Vas, he was four. That's right, isn't it?

SRINIVAS (*uneasy*). Yes.

FRANCES. And when he came to study in England he used to visit all the time. He spent the whole holidays with us once. Richard and I were . . . well, we were like surrogate parents, weren't we? Is that how you would describe it, Vas?

SRINIVAS. Yes. You know, you should finish your drawing. Before the light changes.

FRANCES. That's when we became really close, Vas and I.
Wouldn't you say so, Vas? (*To* JANE.) But you probably
met his mother, didn't you? When you were working at the
shelter?

JANE. I don't think so.

SRINIVAS. My mother doesn't come to the shelter . . .

FRANCES. But she likes to vet your friends, doesn't she?
Especially his girl-friends. She likes to check that he's not
getting too serious.

SRINIVAS. What are you talking about?

FRANCES. You see, that's the thing about these Indian young
men: they're allowed to play the field whilst they're young
but as soon as they hit thirty, wham, they're married off to a
nice Indian girl of good family and good blood. So, you've
got about . . . what? About eighteen months to go, Vas?

SRINIVAS. Why don't you be quiet, Frances?

FRANCES. In fact, I've seen the girl your mother has in mind
for you. She's lovely. Very suitable. Very young.

Silence. FRANCES *takes a drink.* SRINIVAS *is staring at
the table.*

It's very sensible really. We should try it in the West. It might
do something for the divorce rate. But then again, it might
not. It's such a shame that it has to be so complicated – this
marriage business. Isn't it? It's such a shame that we have
this need to attach ourselves to someone else. It would be so
much easier if we just mated and went our separate ways.
I suppose it's because we're insecure. And I suppose that's
because we're too clever, because we know our own fate.
Because we live our whole lives knowing we'll die. And we
know that the only thing that binds us to the earth, that has
any real meaning at all, in the end, is love.

Pause.

I'm going to make some dinner.

She goes inside.

JANE *stands, unsure as to whether she should follow her in.*

SRINIVAS. She's had too much to drink.

JANE *looks unconvinced.*

She hardly ever drinks, but when she does . . .

She is still unconvinced.

What was she talking to you about?

JANE. Her marriage.

SRINIVAS. That's why she's upset then. You're honoured,
    actually. I've never known her to talk about it.

JANE. I think she saw us kiss.

Pause.

SRINIVAS. Yes. Perhaps she did. She's obviously trying to
    warn you about me. Scare you off.

Pause. JANE *is looking increasingly puzzled and concerned.*

Look, Frances is not what she seems. She seems really
composed, really secure, but she's not. Far from it. She's
needy. She needs validation all the time. From men, anyway.
I saw it with her husband. She drove him insane. If she had
given him more space, pulled away from him, he would
have wanted her. Perhaps it's because she was so beautiful
when she was young. Perhaps she's hooked on the attention.
I don't know. But it can be unbearable.

Pause. JANE *is scrutinizing him.*

I suppose she told you he has a 'girlfriend'? But she
probably didn't tell you that the 'girlfriend' is about the
same age as her. She works in television. She's got a better
job than he has.

JANE *is still staring at him. After a moment, she nods, as
though she has understood something. Then she picks up the
bag and starts to go.*

Where are you going?

JANE. Inside.

SRINIVAS. Why? I think we need to talk.

JANE. Not now.

SRINIVAS. Jane, wait. It's not true, what she said. About me getting married.

JANE. It doesn't matter.

SRINIVAS. It does matter. I want it to matter.

JANE. We shouldn't have kissed.

Pause.

We shouldn't have kissed.

Pause.

SRINIVAS. Oh.

JANE. I'm not saying . . . I don't know what I want at the moment. But I just can't . . .

SRINIVAS. Right. It won't happen again then. It was just a kiss. But if it bothers you . . .

JANE. I saw you sitting by my bed. In the shelter. I saw you watching me sleep. I mean I sensed you. I sensed you sitting there. You're important to me. I talk about things with you that I've never talked about with anyone before . . . but . . .

She trails off.

SRINIVAS. Is that why you left the shelter? Tell me it's not.

Pause.

JANE. It was part of it.

He looks away. Anger flashes through him.

SRINIVAS. Do you know where I've been these last few days? Why I didn't come before? I was taking a girl back to her village. A ten-year-old girl with advanced syphilis. She'll be lucky if she survives the year. If she had found her way to the shelter sooner we could have saved her. You could have saved her. That's what we do.

Pause.

You know, you only needed to tell me how you felt and that would have been an end to it. I would have stopped it. Just as I will now. You see, to me, physical intimacy is just another way of connecting with someone. It doesn't mean asking for commitment, or marriage or babies. It's just another profound way of communing with someone else. With someone's Karma. But if you can't see it like that, if you think it would be more complicated, then it probably would be. So it won't happen again. So you see, you can come back to the shelter now, you can come back safe in the knowledge that I'm not going to jump you.

Pause.

Really, I mean it. The only important thing to me is the work. That's all that really matters. And the last thing I would want to do is give you an excuse to run away.

JANE. That's not what I'm doing.

SRINIVAS. Isn't it? What's in the bag, Jane? Another excuse.

She freezes. She is shocked.

I've seen it before: people come out here, thinking they have a vocation, a mission, but as soon as the going gets tough they go running back to their old lives. Happy that they've got something useful on their CV, trying to forget that they ever saw the truth. You have to decide what you want, Jane. You don't even have to come back to the shelter, if you don't trust me. I could find you a placement some-where else. But he's going to be here any minute and he's going to try everything to get you on that plane. So I think you had better decide what your life is for. Don't you?

They stare at each other for a few moments. Then Vas goes inside.

Scene Two

The studio. A spartan room, roughly painted white, with areas of exposed, cracked plaster and a roughly-tiled floor. At one side, a curtained opening leads through to a wash-room, where a sink and water jug are just visible. There are two large windows in the ceiling.

There is an old, leather sofa, extended out to form a small bed. There is a wooden table covered with pots and paints and brushes, and an easel, empty, resting against a wall.

Several completed paintings are leaning against the walls but it is dark in the room – the only light is shed by two candles near to the bed – and the details of the paintings are indistinct.

JANE is sitting on the bed, watching the door. She is wearing a long, Indian-style shirt, by way of a night dress.

Near by, against a wall, is the carrier-bag. On the other side of the bed is MARK's bag and his jacket.

There is some noise outside the room. JANE waits, expectant. A moment later, MARK enters. On seeing her, he stops abruptly. He stares at her.

MARK. She said I could sleep in here.

JANE. I don't have to stay.

   Pause.

   He comes further into the room and puts his bag down. Now that he is in the light, it is possible to see that he has a cut nose and lip and a great deal of blood on his face and shirt.

   What happened to you? God, what happened . . .

MARK. I fell off that bike. That bike. I fell off it.

JANE. Mark.

MARK. The light gave up on me. It worked for about five minutes then it just faded out. Useless! What's the point of having a light if it doesn't work?

JANE (*getting up*). Here – sit down.

He does so.

MARK. There are no street lights out there. It's pitch dark.

JANE is examining his face.

I must have hit a stone. I went straight over the handle-bars. I think I was unconscious for a minute.

JANE. Wait there.

She takes a candle through to the washroom. She fills a bowl of water from a jug.

MARK takes his bloody shirt off.

She returns, with the water, some tissues and a towel. She sets it down next to him and begins to clean the cuts on his face.

MARK. This Indian bloke came along in a cart. Some sort of cow pulling it. He helped me sort the bike out.

JANE. Good.

MARK. He had this plastic bottle with water in. He tipped some over my face, got some of the dirt off.

JANE. That's good.

MARK. Yes. He was trying to get me to drink some but I didn't want to risk it. You're not supposed to drink the water unless it's been boiled, are you?

JANE. It was probably Evian.

MARK. Yes.

Pause.

He was kind.

She stops what she's doing and looks at him.

JANE. That's good.

MARK. Yes. He laughed a lot, actually. At me, you know. He had this really good laugh. Rotten teeth, but a good laugh. Infectious.

JANE. Yes. Are you hurt anywhere else?

MARK. Not really. I think my knees are bruised.

He hold up his hands, which are grazed and dirty.

JANE. Just a moment.

She takes the bowl back to the washroom and changes the water.

She returns.

JANE. Wash your hands in there.

He does so.

MARK. I think there's a tube of cream in one of my pockets. You know, the one we use for Joe.

JANE. Right.

She goes to where his jacket is lying over his bag, and searches. She moves a candle so as to see better and light is thrown onto one of the paintings. It is a well-executed, stylised portrait of SRINIVAS. MARK *sees it.*

MARK. What's that?

JANE. One of her paintings. There are more over there.

MARK. Isn't that . . . ?

JANE. Yes. They're all of Vas.

She brings out a tube of antiseptic cream. She takes it over to MARK *and begins applying it to his cuts and bruises.*

MARK. God. Do you think they're just friends?

JANE. No. I don't.

MARK. God.

Pause.

God. She's old enough to be his mother.

Pause. She continues to apply the antiseptic.

JANE. I was getting worried about you.

Pause.

MARK. Perhaps you'll know how it feels now.

She takes this in, but doesn't respond. She takes his hands and gently dries each one, applies the cream. He watches her. She finishes off and holds both his hands in her own for a moment.

JANE. There. You'll live.

Their eyes meet for a moment. Then she puts his hands down gently. She wipes her hands on the towel. She pushes the bowl aside. She is kneeling in front of him. They sit in silence for a few moments.

Did you manage to speak to him?

MARK. Yes. He's all right. He was watching a new video. He didn't want to talk for long. I told him I'd seen you.

JANE. What did he say?

MARK. He asked if you'd got him a present. He asked if you were coming home. I said you are. Soon.

Pause.

You are coming home, aren't you?

Pause.

JANE. Mark . . .

MARK. No, wait. I've got something to say. I've listened to what you've said, now you can listen to me. I've thought about what you said: about how I think about Joe all the time. About how I don't have hopes for myself any more . . . ambitions . . .

JANE. Mark . . .

MARK. No, wait. I'm talking now. After Joe was born, I said to you – do you remember – after everyone had stopped coming round and there was just all those nights, those nights without sleeping and his feeding trouble and everything – I said to you then, we're in this together. I'm not going to be the sort of dad who ignores his kid until

he's old enough to play football. We're in this together. And
I reckon I've been there for you . . .

JANE. You have . . .

MARK. Wait. I know I work a lot. But I am there, aren't I, at
weekends and that? I know I play football on a Sunday but
apart from that?

JANE. Yes.

MARK. I know my job's not great. I know I'll probably never
get anywhere, or make a lot of money. But I work really
hard, for you and for Joe. And if that makes me a failure in
your eyes, well . . .

JANE. It doesn't. I don't think you're a failure, I've never
thought that. I'm proud of you. So proud of you. You look
after us so well . . .

MARK. So what's the problem then? I don't really get it.
What's the problem? I know I worry about Joe, but you
have to worry. It's a bad world. Christ, there are so many
things that could go wrong.

JANE. But sometimes it seems like that's all we ever think
about – the things that can go wrong.

MARK. But we have to . . .

JANE. It's like we're in hiding the whole time. Running away
instead of facing it . . .

MARK. Think about where you were brought up – drug
pushers living next door, muggings, rapes in the stair-wells.

JANE. I know, but . . .

MARK. I don't want Joe to have to see those things. I don't
want him anywhere near those things. All right? So if that
means me working hard, if that means me worrying about
him, that's what I'll do.

Pause.

I want the best for him. What's wrong with that. Eh? I want
what any parent wants for their kid. I want him to do well

at school. I want him to go to college. I want him to get a good job. I want him to do better than us, better than my mum and dad . . .

JANE. Why?

MARK. Why? Why what?

JANE. Why do you want him to do better?

MARK. Why? Because. You know why. Because. Because I don't want him to have to worry like we worry. You're the one who's going on about me worrying. I want him to have opportunities. I want him to be able to have what he wants: have a holiday when he wants a holiday, have a Lambourghini if he wants a Lambourghini.

JANE. And you think that would make him happy? Having a Lambourghini?

MARK. Well, it would make me happy! Everyone wants more than they've got. It's not news. Ask anyone. Ask your woman in the hut with the flies and the baby. Just because we can't all have it, doesn't mean it's wrong to want it. And if I can get my son ahead of the game, I'm sorry, but I'll do it.

Pause.

JANE. The game?

MARK. Yes, the game. Oh, for Christ's sake, Jane, it's just a figure of speech.

JANE. Why does he have to play the game at all? Why don't we teach him to question the game? To change the game?

MARK. Oh, don't be stupid. The game's the game, isn't it? It's life. It's life.You work to make money so's to eat. To survive. To put a roof over your head.

JANE. It's not about surviving. Not any more. It's about having a load of things we don't even need. Having them so that someone else can't have them.

MARK. Oh, here we go!

JANE. There's enough food in the world to feed everyone five times over. No one in this world needs to be hungry.

MARK. Where did you read that? On one of your leaflets?

JANE. We should be changing the way the world works. The whole way society is.

MARK. Oh for God's sake! Listen to yourself. You may as well go and join those morons smashing up McDonalds and shouting about capitalism!

JANE. Maybe I should.

MARK. What do you want us to do? Drop out? Go and live on a commune in Wales and make sandals out of . . . stuff . . . straw? Turn into hippies? Start travelling?

JANE. That seems so ridiculous does it?

MARK. Yes, it does. It does seem ridiculous. It is ridiculous!

JANE. More ridiculous than what we do now? Running around like maniacs, you working every hour God sends, never stopping, never . . .

MARK. We have holidays.

JANE. Yes, we save up every penny we've got to go away once a year and even that just turns into a big worry. Worrying about whether the flights will be delayed, you charging about complaining about the food and the safety in the swimming pool and what's included in the all included.

MARK. Oh, thanks. Thanks a lot. That's the last time I take you on holiday.

JANE. You're always angry about something. You're always stressed. You're always worried. We don't listen to each other, we don't talk to each other . . .

MARK. Well you try working as hard as I work!

JANE. I don't want Joe to grow up like that. I don't want that to be his life. It hasn't made us happy, why should it make him happy?

MARK. Because he'd be better at it!

JANE. No. No, Mark.

MARK. Anyway, who says we're not happy? Eh? I'm happy. I'm very happy.

JANE. How can you say that?

MARK. Because I am.

JANE. Well I'm not. I'm not happy. With any of it!

There is a long silence. MARK *shakes his head. Then silence again.*

MARK. Is this why you don't want another kid?

JANE. Yes.

MARK. So all that stuff you used to come out with about wanting to go and do some exams or something, that was just an excuse was it? That was lies was it?

Pause.

JANE. When I think about having another kid . . .

Pause.

MARK. What?

JANE. It's like when you're travelling on a train, and you see a beautiful little house, with swings in the garden . . . and a conservatory . . . and you think, I wish that was mine. But then you realise that because you're there, sitting on the train looking at it, well . . . it means it wouldn't be a nice place to be. It wouldn't be idyllic. With trains thundering past. People staring. It's ruined. They're all ruined.

Long pause.

MARK. I don't know. I don't know what to say to you, Jane. I just don't know. I don't even feel like I know you any more.

JANE. I tell you what I really wish we did sometimes.

MARK. What?

JANE. Prayed.

MARK. Jesus!

JANE. Not to God, it doesn't have to be to God. I mean I just wish we would sometimes sit down together and . . . and just accept that there's something bigger than us. And that we don't really know what we're doing. Just really think about how we could be better, and about how we could help Joe to see the world more . . . more honestly.

MARK *covers his face with his hands.*

I mean, there doesn't seem to be any thoughtfulness any more. It's just one big free-for-all, one big grab-bag. I wish we could sometimes just sit and be grateful for all the good things in our lives. Just enjoy the fact that Joe is there. Just enjoy each other.

Pause.

MARK. We could always have sex.

JANE *suddenly starts to cry. Big sobs.*

It was only a joke. God. It was only a joke. Don't cry. Come on. Don't cry. What, it's that bad a prospect is it? Come on. It was only a joke. What are you crying for? Come on.

JANE. It's sad. It's so sad.

MARK. What? What is?

JANE. I can't come back with you.

Pause.

MARK. No. Don't say that. You can. You can come back.

JANE. I can't.

MARK. You can. Look. Look, it was only a joke. I'll try, I'll try to do what you want me to do. You just say it and I'll do it. Maybe not the sandals in Wales . . . but . . . Look, this is just because you're here. Because you've had such a weird time. If you come home, we'll be able to sort it out . . .

JANE. It wouldn't work.

MARK. It would.

JANE. We'd just end up how we were before.

MARK. No. No, I mean it. I could try to change.

JANE. I can't make you do what you don't want. I can't make you feel something if you don't feel it.

MARK. Look, all this is just so much talk. It's not like there's anything really wrong. Anything serious. We can sort it out. The only thing that matters is whether we love each other. Because I really love you, Jane. And you love me, don't you? Eh? Don't you?

JANE. Yes.

MARK. Well then.

JANE. It's not that simple.

MARK. Would you choose me, eh? That is the question, isn't it, eh? Would you choose me? Because I'd choose you. If you were in a huge room with a thousand other women, even really gorgeous ones, I'd still choose you. Would you choose me? Eh?

Pause.

JANE. I don't know. I don't know if I would.

MARK (*covering the panic*). Well, I'd have to volunteer then, wouldn't I? You know, (*Raising his hand.*) 'I'm Spartacus', do you remember that? (*Hugging her.*) Come here. Come here. I've missed you.

JANE. Oh God . . .

MARK. I need you. I need you so much. We're a family. You and me and Joe. That's all that matters. That we're there for him. That we're there for each other. That's all that matters. That's all. That's all.

Scene Three

The living room. SRINIVAS *is waiting, agitated.* FRANCES *enters from the direction of the stairs.*

She has changed into her nightdress and let her hair down. She looks lovely.

SRINIVAS. Is he still in there?

FRANCES. Yes. I don't think he'll be coming out of there tonight, so you may as well go.

Pause.

SRINIVAS. You know, bitterness is extremely unattractive.

FRANCES. I suppose you've been telling her to stay, have you? Telling her to stay here and change the world with you? That would suit you very well, wouldn't it? A pretty little white girl running around after you, hanging on your every word. You wouldn't have to bother with me any more. You know, it's rather suspect, your penchant for white women. British women. You must really want to get one over on the old Empire. Or is that you can't quite get beyond the idea that a pale face is more desirable than a dark one?

SRINIVAS. Why don't you shut-up, Frances!

FRANCES. Hit a nerve, have I?

SRINIVAS. What on earth is wrong with you? You should hear yourself. I have been telling her to stay, but not for my sake . . .

FRANCES. Oh.

SRINIVAS. For her sake. Because I know she won't be happy if she goes back. Because she's too honest. Because she's almost, almost able to make the step that she wants to make . . .

FRANCES. She's a recruit!

SRINIVAS. Yes. If you like. I'm not going to apologise for that.

FRANCES. A recruit you'll enjoy screwing occasionally, in those rare, rare moments when you feel a little lonely.

SRINIVAS. Don't be so base.

FRANCES. Base? Oh, of course, because you're above normal emotions, aren't you? Good old every day needs. That's why you come running to me three times a week. Even Mother Teresa had her faith, Vas.

SRINIVAS. Meaning what?

FRANCES. And don't say it's because you feel sorry for me. Don't say it's compassion because you haven't got a compassionate bone in your body. I've watched you all day with that man, that poor, poor man who thought his wife might be dead . . .

SRINIVAS. Oh please . . .

FRANCES. That poor man who just wants to take his son's mother back home and you haven't even been able to show him respect, let alone understanding.

SRINIVAS. I didn't notice much respect coming from him.

FRANCES. He's in a strange country.

SRINIVAS. He's a racist bully.

FRANCES. He's worried. He's afraid.

SRINIVAS. That's none of my concern.

FRANCES. No, no, of course it isn't. I suppose that's just sentiment, isn't it?

SRINIVAS. It's entirely up to her to decide how much he means to her. It's not my responsibility.

FRANCES. And what about her son? Taking her from her son, is that your responsibility?

SRINIVAS. No. It isn't. Anyway, I told her she can bring him here if she wants to.

FRANCES. It's quite amazing. You work all day to help children with no parents and yet you're quite prepared to take her away from her own child.

SRINIVAS. They're two completely different things.

FRANCES. How? How?

SRINIVAS. I'm not in the business of compassion. I don't help
the children because I feel sorry for them, I help them
because they have rights – the right to an education, the
right . . .

FRANCES (*speaking over him*). You don't need to lecture me,
Vas.

SRINIVAS. . . . not to be forced to work, the right not to be
abused. I'm sure her son would have all those things, even
without her.

FRANCES. But he wouldn't have a mother. Or does that not
matter? The happiness of one little child in the West?

SRINIVAS. All the children matter. It's what's best for all the
children.

Pause.

FRANCES. What if she's ill?

SRINIVAS. What do you mean?

FRANCES. What if she's mentally ill?

SRINIVAS. She's not.

FRANCES. You don't know that. She's clearly been going
through some sort of depression . . .

SRINIVAS. She just reached a crisis point. She needed to
change her life and the reality of it was overwhelming. The
baby thing is just her way of playing for time. It's a get-out.
I told her that.

FRANCES. You told her?

SRINIVAS. Yes.

Pause.

FRANCES. And what if she couldn't adjust? What if her
depression got worse, would you look after her?

Pause.

If she'd been working with you for a few weeks and she suddenly broke down again? Started crying again? Stopped talking. Would you look after her?

SRINIVAS. Yes.

FRANCES. God, Vas, you really are . . .

SRINIVAS. I do care, Frances. I'm perfectly capable of caring, as long as it's helpful. And constructive. Anyway, I think we should stop pretending that this is a moral issue, don't you?

Pause.

It's unbelievable. One kiss, just one kiss and this is what happens.

FRANCES. What? What happens?

SRINIVAS. This. This demeaning display of jealousy.

The word demeaning seems to really hurt her.

There is nothing going on between myself and Jane. Nothing. I want her to stay and work at the shelter. She was a good worker. We need people like her. I thought you believed in my work. Frances?

FRANCES. I do. I do.

SRINIVAS. Well then.

Silence.

FRANCES. It's very hard; being so low down on everyone's list of priorities.

SRINIVAS. When are you going to stop feeling sorry for yourself? Playing the martyr gains you nothing. There's no-one watching, Frances. There's no music playing under your sad moments. There's no one appreciating the real you. There's no-one there.

Pause.

FRANCES. Thanks.

SRINIVAS. You know, one of my earliest memories is of you. I must have been about seven. You were the shining lady.

You overflowed with life. You said, 'Come on, tidy boy, we're going to do some painting.' You spread some paper out on the floor, a sheet so big that it filled the room. We held down the edges with pieces of furniture. Then we stepped through paint in our bare feet, and we danced. All over the paper. We danced like furies. Then we hung out our dance on the washing line and watched it moving in the wind. Do you remember that?

FRANCES. Yes.

SRINIVAS. You're wasting your life.

Pause.

FRANCES. I'll tell you what really kills me . . . what really kills me is when I let my stupid, pathetic imagination start thinking of how I would like us to be. How I'd like you to search out my face when you walk in a room. How I'd like you to protect me. How you'd worry about me. How I'd like you to kiss me in front of everyone and be proud of me.

SRINIVAS. If you want those things, you should go out and find someone who can give them to you.

Pause.

I didn't ask you to come out here.

FRANCES. No.

He comes over to her. He leans over her back and kisses her neck, runs his hands over her breasts. A shiver runs through her. She stares into the space around her.

SRINIVAS. If this is hurting you, Frances, stop it.

Scene Four

The studio. Night. MARK *and* JANE *are asleep on the sofa-bed.*

JANE *is having a nightmare.*

JANE. No. No. Don't. Get off. Get off . . .

She is trembling violently and drenched in sweat. She whines out –

Oh no, oh no. Oh no, please, no . . .

MARK *wakes up.*

No. Get off. Get off me . . .

MARK. Jane?

JANE. Oh no, please . . . oh no, oh no . . .

MARK. Jane?

He is unsure what to do – whether to try to wake her or let it run its course.

I'm here, Jane. It's all right. It's a dream . . .

She suddenly sits up and starts screaming over and over.

(*Shouting and shaking her.*) Jane! Jane! Jane!

She awakens. She looks at him.

It's me. It's Mark. You're all right. It was a dream. You're all right. It's all right.

She begins to cry.

It's all right now. It's all right.

JANE. The baby.

He holds her and rocks her.

MARK. It's all right.

JANE. The baby.

MARK. You were dreaming. There's no baby. It's all right now.

JANE. I killed it.

MARK. No. No, you didn't. It was a dream. There's no baby. There's no baby.

JANE. There is.

MARK. No. No.

She breaks from his embrace and looks into his eyes with absolute conviction and horror.

JANE. There is. There is.

FRANCES arrives at the open door.

FRANCES. Is she all right?

MARK. Come in a minute.

She enters, still tying her robe, a little breathless from hurrying.

FRANCES. Was it a nightmare? She's had a few since she came here.

MARK. She says there's a baby.

FRANCES. What?

SRINIVAS appears in the doorway, a sheet tied around his waist.

MARK. She says there is a baby. She says she killed it.

FRANCES. She's dreaming.

MARK. No. No, she means it.

JANE. I killed it.

Pause. FRANCES and MARK are unable to speak.

SRINIVAS (*entering the room*). What do you mean, Jane?

JANE. The woman in the shanty town, with the thin baby.
I gave her my passport and my keys and my rings and she gave me her baby. And it tucked itself into my neck, like a

tiny bat. And I started to walk. I walked and walked to find
a safe place for the baby, because I have to take care of this
baby. It's dark, it's night and now there are people behind
me. There are people. They're following me through the
streets. And I walk faster and I almost drop the baby and
I put it into my bag to keep it safe. And I run. And I reach
a shore. It is the sea. And now I can see them. They're
coming from the darkness. They're boys. They're only boys.
Each one's older than the one before. They're begging from
me – 'Medam Medam, Medam Medam'. They're running
around me. They're excited. Their eyes are shining. They're
laughing and doing somersaults. And they start to touch me,
tugging at my sleeves, just touching, slightly, 'Medam
Medam'. 'I can't,' I say, 'I've got nothing'. 'Medam
Medam,' they tap their mouths. They point down into their
throats, their throats are like caves. They pull at me now,
'Medam Medam'. I lift the bag above my head to keep the
baby safe. I'm panicking – 'I've got nothing', they love it,
my fear, it's thrilling them. The youngest one's on the
ground, he has his hands around my legs, 'Medam Medam'.
I drag him, with every step I drag him along the sand. He's
laughing, the older boys are laughing, pulling at my skin
and hair. I try to get his fingers off my ankles but they 're so
strong, they're strong with need. 'Get off me. Get off me'.
I free my leg, my leg's free and I kick, I kick his head, hard.
I kick. His fingers come off me. He falls back. There's
nothing. There's shock. Then he smiles, and sits up and rubs
his head, like he's in a cartoon and the boys laugh and laugh
and I run. I run fast, with the bag against my chest. And
when I stop it 's almost light and I'm in a square. And I sit
on the ground, the stone ground, and I open up the bag and
I put my hand inside to take out the baby, the baby . . . but
it is dead. It's dry and hard and flat. It's dead.

She is shaking violently. MARK *is unable to move.*
FRANCES *is crying silently.*

SRINIVAS *walks forward. He picks up the plastic bag and
takes it to* JANE. *He kneels down beside her. He takes*
JANE's *hand in his own and reaches down into the bag.
They pull out an open brown envelope.* JANE *stares at it,*

with a vague sense of recognition. SRINIVAS *reaches into it and brings out a passport, and a wedding ring, and some money.*

They are silent for several moments.

JANE *reaches out and takes the passport. She opens it and looks at the picture of herself.*

She wouldn't take them. I remember . . . I held them out to her. She started shouting at me. She thought I was trying to buy her baby. She wouldn't let him go. Not for my whole world. Not for my whole world.

ACT THREE

Scene One

The garden. Early morning. JANE *is standing by the table. She is looking for a number on* SRINIVAS*'s mobile phone.*

SRINIVAS *enters.* JANE *sees him.*

JANE. You don't mind, do you?

SRINIVAS. Of course not.

JANE. I need to phone a taxi. I thought you might have a number in here.

SRINIVAS. I haven't. Frances will have a number somewhere. Where are you going?

She doesn't answer.

Come on, Jane. Lets see if you can look me in the eye and say it.

JANE (*looking him in the eye*). I'm going back home. With Mark.

Pause. SRINIVAS *comes and sits down at the table. He stares out at the garden.*

SRINIVAS. Your magnolia has bloomed.

JANE. Yes.

Pause.

I have to go back.

SRINIVAS. I don't want to hear it.

JANE. But things are going to be different.

SRINIVAS. I don't want to hear it.

JANE (*forcefully*). I want you to hear it. I never told him how I was feeling, before I left, I never tried to explain it to him because . . . I don't know . . . I don't know if I could have explained. I suppose I thought he wouldn't understand.

SRINIVAS. And now you've told him and he understands it all. Perfectly.

JANE. He wants to understand. I have to give him a chance, give us a chance, I owe him that.

SRINIVAS. You don't owe him anything.

JANE. He's my husband. I owe him something, don't I? I mean isn't that part of what's wrong with the world? We think we owe nothing to anyone?

Pause.

SRINIVAS. Possibly.

JANE. We're going to work at living in a way that . . . that I can live with. He says he's going to really try. I don't know how we're going to do it. We'll start with the small things. If it doesn't work . . . if it really can't work, then I'll have to . . . to think again. But I've got to give it a chance.

Pause.

SRINIVAS. Here's a scenario for you. You go back. It's all right for a month. Maybe two. He's just relieved that you're home. He listens to you. He tries to be open to your ideas. He tries not to smirk when you suggest, what? Helping out in a soup kitchen every other Sunday? Switching off the telly once a week and talking about spirituality? Helping your son to choose some toys to donate to the local children's home? Are those the sort of things? And then the shock and the emotions of the last few weeks start to wear off. He starts to think about how he behaved out here and he starts to feel a little foolish. He starts to feel he was manipulated and he feels angry with you for that. He starts blocking your suggestions. He gets back-up from his parents and his football chums. He wears you down. And you don't want to rock the boat again. Your son is just getting used to having you back, so you bite your tongue. Over and over and over again you bite your tongue. And one day you wake up and you decide that it's better to just tow the line. Better for everyone. Smoother. And you can still give your ten pounds at Christmas. And that's something, isn't it?

JANE. It's not going to be like that.

SRINIVAS. Yes it is.

JANE. If it gets like that, I'll leave.

SRINIVAS. He won't let you leave. Not this time.

JANE. I'll leave.

SRINIVAS. He's never going to let go of you. He'll undermine you, stupefy you. He'll break down your confidence so you feel like you can't leave.

JANE. Stop it!

Pause.

I'm going back. I have to see Joe. I should never have left him.

SRINIVAS. I told you, go and get him. Bring him out here.

JANE. I have to think about what's best for him. He's my responsibility. The woman in the shanty-town was right. You should never let go of your kids. They're the most important thing. If I leave Joe, Mark will bring him up exactly how he wants to. I've got to stay with him. I've got to bring him up with the truth. Isn't that just as important as coming here and working at the shelter? Isn't that how it has to start?

SRINIVAS. No. You can't do that. You can't just pass the buck. 'Leave it to the next generation, we'll educate them, they'll make the changes'. It has to start with you. What you do. What he sees you do. That's how it starts. You think that dream, that delusion you had was about Joe, don't you? About your abandoning Joe?

JANE. Yes.

SRINIVAS. It wasn't. Think about it. It was about taking responsibility for someone else's child. The fear that you might find it too hard. It's because you were starting to take responsibility for the children in the shelter, on the streets. And that's good. Because it is a responsibility. That's how you have to see it. That's how the world has to see it. Not as an affair of the heart – 'that news report made me cry today so I'll give them some money, tomorrow I'll forget them again.' A responsibility. And you can do it.

JANE. I kicked that boy, Vas. I know I didn't . . . I know I didn't take the baby, but there were some boys. And I did kick him.

SRINIVAS. Other people's need can be terrifying. It can be cynical, merciless. It can feel as though it is eating your very soul. Do you think there aren't moments when I just want to tell those kids, everyone, anyone to get out of my face? It's primal – If I look after him, who's going to look after me? Or who's going to watch my back? But it passes. Our heads take over. Our thoughts kick in. It passes. You're not a saint. Saints don't exist. You're just a woman doing her best.

He puts his hand on her face.

You're so close, Jane . . .

MARK *enters. He sees them. He tenses up.*

MARK. Have you called?

Pause.

JANE. No.

Pause.

SRINIVAS. She's not sure if she's going.

MARK. What?

SRINIVAS. She's not sure if she's going.

MARK. What have you said to her?

SRINIVAS. Nothing that she didn't know already . . .

MARK. What have you said to her? Jesus Christ, what is it with you? Who are you?

MARK is approaching SRINIVAS. FRANCES enters and watches in amazement.

I mean, what is it you want from us? What is it with you? Why are you trying to split us up? Eh? What is it you want?

SRINIVAS. I just want . . .

MARK. You want to get into her knickers. Is that it?

He has reached him. He starts pushing him, goading him.

SRINIVAS. Oh, please . . .

MARK. Is that what you want? Is that what you want? Make her think you're the good guy so she'll come quietly. Eh? Is that it? You dirty, filthy little . . .

MARK hits SRINIVAS. SRINIVAS retaliates. They start to fight.

FRANCES. Stop it!

They continue to fight. JANE turns her back on them and sits down on a chair. The two men gradually lose momentum. SRINIVAS realises how humiliating this is. MARK runs out of emotional energy. The fight fizzles out.

Long pause.

JANE. Vas, would you go and get me the number for the taxi, please.

He doesn't move.

Please.

He looks into her eyes for several moments. Then, reluctantly, he goes.

Pause.

Go and get our things, Mark.

MARK. You are coming? Aren't you?

JANE. Go and get our things.

MARK. Yes.

Pause

Yes.

He goes. JANE *sits down. She is shaking. Pause.*

FRANCES. Morning.

JANE *manages half a smile. It breaks the tension slightly.*

Pause.

JANE. I have to see Joe, Frances.

FRANCES. Yes.

JANE. Vas doesn't understand that. He hasn't got children. He doesn't understand that.

FRANCES. No.

JANE. But he's right, about so many things.

Pause.

What if he's right?

Pause.

FRANCES. Vas is very persuasive. He's a very clever young man and he has a lot of brilliant ideas. But he does change his mind about things. I'm not saying that he's a hypocrite because he's not. He always believes passionately in what he says and he will always, I think, want to change the world for the better. But I remember a time when he used to say that there was no point working on the ground, that charity work was a waste of time, that one had to go into big business and change things by showing that business can be ethical.

JANE *looks at her in surprise.* FRANCES *nods.*

And I remember when he decided that Art was the only way to change things and he was going to become a film-maker. And then he started saying that he had to do charity work so that he could argue from a position of experience. Don't do

anything because Vas thinks it's right. It's your life; do it if
you think it's right.

Pause.

Vas will be Vas. He'll move on. In two years time from
now, I doubt if he'll even be at the shelter. He'll probably
have gone into politics. He'll probably be running the
country. Lets just hope he learns to love along the way.

Pause.

JANE. You and Vas . . .

FRANCES *shakes her head.*

FRANCES. There isn't. There isn't me and Vas. Not because
of you.

Pause.

I thought I needed him. I do need him. It's got to stop.

Pause.

JANE. What will you do?

FRANCES. I'm not quite sure. Yet. Go home and see my boys.
Sort out the divorce. I'll find something different to paint,
that's for sure.

JANE *smiles.*

There's a lady; a round, matronly, lovely lady, who goes
around India with an entourage. And people queue up for
hours and hours and when they finally get to see her, all
they want from her is a hug. She's supposed to have a hot-
line to the Gods and it's supposed to be divinely comforting,
this hug. So perhaps I'll go and find her. See if she can
satisfy me.

She smiles at JANE

Or perhaps I'll ask if she wants an understudy.

*They laugh and then they hug. For a long time. Then, as
they are hugging,* JANE *says*

JANE. Frances?

FRANCES. Yes.

JANE. Is there a back gate?

> FRANCES *lets go of her and looks at her.*

From the garden. Is there a back gate?

Pause.

FRANCES. They'll come after you.

> *They stare at each other, frozen to the spot.* JANE*'s heart is pounding. She is ready to go.*

> MARK *and* SRINIVAS *enter. They stand awkwardly, slightly apart from each other, but still together.*

SRINIVAS. We were just saying . . . we were just saying . . . perhaps I should drive you into town. You and Mark. We could call at the shelter before we go to the airport. You could say goodbye to some of the children. And you could show Mark where you've been working for the last few weeks.

> *Pause.* JANE *looks at* MARK.

MARK. Yes. It might help. For me to see. What do you think?

> JANE *is staring at them. There are tears in her eyes. Eventually, she nods.*

JANE. Yes. That might help.

> *Long pause. They stand. Unable to move.*

SRINIVAS. Right then.

> *They still cannot move.*

FRANCES. You know, after we left India, my family lived in Russia for a while. They have a tradition there, where before they go on a journey, they all sit down, with their coats and hats on, with their bags and things and they sit for two minutes and think; about the journey ahead of them, about where they are in the world. Where they're going. Perhaps we should do that.

> *Pause.*

SRINIVAS. Yes. Perhaps we should.

JANE. Yes.

Pause.

MARK. Just sit and think?

FRANCES. Yes.

Pause.

MARK. Right then.

He looks at JANE.

JANE. Right then.

They sit in the chairs around the table. The lights start to go down. Gradually they take each other's hands. MARK last. The lights fade out.

End.

80

Mother Teresa is Dead first published in Great Britain in 2002
as a paperback original by Nick Hern Books Ltd, 14 Larden Road,
London W3 7ST, in association with the Royal Court Theatre, London

Mother Teresa is Dead copyright © 2002 by Helen Edmundson

Helen Edmundson has asserted her moral right to be identified
as the author of this work

Typeset by Country Setting, Kingsdown, Kent CT14 8ES
Printed by Bookmarque, Croydon, Surrey

A CIP catalogue record for this book is available from
the British Library

ISBN 1 85459 700 0